Dancing in my Nightgown

Dancing in my Nightgown

The Rhythms of Widowhood

Betty Auchard

Stephens Press ✷ Las Vegas, Nevada

Editing: Sandra Knauke, Photography: (jacket) Fred Armitage/Visual
Impact, (interior) Paul Becker, Renee Ray, Betty Auchard, Carol Wood,
Design: Sue Campbell

ISBN 1-932173-45-5

CIP Data Available

Stephens
Press LLC

A Stephens Media Group Company

Post Office Box 1600
Las Vegas, NV 89125-1600

www.stephenspress.com

Printed in Hong Kong

For Denny

I'm passionate about many things, especially dancing. I dance alone in my nightgown to smooth jazz playing on the radio while the coffee is brewing. It's like going to church.

— Betty Auchard

Contents

Part 3—**Staying Afloat**

Part 4—**Moving On**

Part 5—**The New Me**

Part 6—**Ready For Romance**

Epilogue

Acknowledgements

I wish to thank SO many people who have supported my new writing journey, that I'm afraid of leaving someone out. So whoever you might be . . . forgive me.

First, I want to acknowledge my four children, Dave, Dodie, Renee, Bob, and their families who have always been an integral part of my life experiences. Next was Maryann Gravitt, artist/editor of the Volcano, CA Newsletter, who published my essays, poems, and short stories for five years. Those publications alone helped qualify me as an active member of South Bay California Writers Club (CWC), another group to whom I'm *deeply* indebted. Sonja Larsen, my artist friend from Minnesota, was one of the first readers I provided with an ongoing stream of stories — and the person who suggested I submit my work to Kay Allenbaugh, editor of the Chocolate for a Woman's Soul series by Simon & Schuster. Thus began my fondness for seeing my efforts in print because that publisher eventually included five of my tales in their anthologies. Kay's administrative assistant, Jan Richardson, in turn, advised that I pull it all together as a presentation for her Business Women's Forum of Tigard, OR, and that's when I remembered how much I loved an audience. I didn't know those women were giving me a standing ovation; I thought they were stretching their legs to clap.

In an online writing group, my path crossed with my future editor and writing partner from Nebraska, Sandi Corbitt-Sears. (sandi@writefriend. com). Soon, Bruce McAllister (www.geocities.com/bhmcallister) joined us. He was my writing coach at a CWC conference in Pacific Grove, CA. These two people (gifts from nowhere) have been significant elements of my professional team for over five years. I love them and I'm beholden for their expertise with the written word and for validating the worth of my stories. Because of Sandi and Bruce, I developed more than blind faith in myself. I learned how to write better and how to prepare for agents and publishers, which eventually allowed me to share this book with the public.

Next, there was Susan Letham, a key writing instructor who I've never met but who I know well. She taught me more than I ever dreamed I could learn in her online writing workshops at Insprired2write.com. She kept me moving forward, learning the intricacies of word-weaving in nine different workshops in two years. Finally, Susan wrote for all of the class to read, "Betty, stop taking classes and start writing." I always do as the teacher asks which is another reason that you're reading this page.

And while all of this exciting writing was happening, the dishes piled up in the sink and the dust bunnies held conventions in the corners of every room in my home. Naturally I wrote about it. And I pressed stories onto everyone I knew, especially the women in my neighborhood. I wrote about them, too. Those sweet honeys are my largest fan club. And I blossomed in the memoir classes I took at the Willows Senior Center in San Jose, CA under the tutelage of Ann Thompson, a most able teacher. Another memoir class at the Kirk Senior Center in San Jose under the leadership of Lynn Rodgers, accomplished writer and instructor, was equally inspiring. Feedback from other students was invaluable and stories I wrote in both classes got published in places beyond my Christmas letters.

Finally, only I know how greatly the following people facilitated my writing journey by laughing, crying, suggesting, protesting, and ultimately accepting my tales: Al Adams (teacher, treasured friend), Paul Becker (photographer with great ideas), Connie Dulany (closest wise-woman-pal), Don Elarton (cherished cousin-once-removed, Laura Ingles Wilder authority), Carol Johnson-Davis (bereavement counselor, artist, collaborator), Joanne Rafferty (bereavement counselor, supporter), Basil Stevens (writing buddy, fan, now applauding from heaven), Ken Watkins (bereavement counselor, ally), Carol Wood (more than just my webmistress), my water aerobics class, the staff at Copy Max on Blossom Hill Road in San Jose, the team at Stephens Press, my siblings, Pat Reffel and Bob Peal, who cheerfully read early drafts of my stories, and Custom Seams of Los Gatos, CA, for creating the silk nightgown on the cover; I thank you all . . . so much.

Betty Auchard

Introduction

*I*n 1997, my husband, Denny, was diagnosed with a fast-growing cancer that started in his lungs and invaded the rest of his body. His symptoms were so dramatic that he had to be hospitalized for ten days before aggressive chemotherapy could even be started. His prognosis was not hopeful, for we learned there was no cure. Our lives were turned upside-down. I felt that two trains had flattened me — one was cancer and the other was Denny's approaching death.

I spent each day at the hospital and went home each night and shut the windows and howled a wild primal cry as I stood naked under the shower. I knelt at the side of my bed wailing, not knowing what words to say except, "Help us, help us." But I returned to the hospital daily and wore a brave face and wondered if Denny could tell that my eyes were swollen. If he did, he never mentioned it. He was too busy trying to persuade his bloated limbs to move so he could get out of bed every fifteen minutes to pee. He refused to give up and focused all of his energy on staying alive. I was torn between believing him or the doctors who said that he would be lucky if he had twelve months left to be with us.

And the doctors were right. Denny died on July 9, 1998, almost ten months after he was diagnosed with cancer.

After Denny died, I needed to talk. Since there wasn't always someone to listen, I started to write on anything that would take the mark of a pencil. That scribbling became my tool for healing. I grieved, I laughed, and I wrote so I wouldn't forget what it was like. Writing affirmed that I was alive and that my experiences were important. To my surprise, that writing became a vital connection to others who were alone.

Dancing in my Nightgown is a collection of the stories I wrote after Denny's death. They show how I dealt with the life-altering experience of losing my life partner and what I did to start over. I learned to embrace the rhythms of widowhood, which wasn't easy, and I finally realized that my old life was over. Nothing would ever be the same again. It took a few years, but I came to view widowhood as an opportunity to find out what I could do on my own.

I had more to learn than most women. I had never been single before. I was barely nineteen when I married Denny, an old man of twenty-three, and I went straight from my parents' home to my husband's bed.

After Denny died, I had to find out how to put gasoline in our car. I was not freeway literate nor had I ever used a computer. Income taxes were what other people did, and I'd never paid the bills myself.

When I looked at a billing statement, I didn't know what a minus sign by the "amount due" meant. Some amounts due were mysteriously higher each month, but I paid them anyway. When I finally called, my cell phone company said I was so far ahead that I didn't need to pay the bill for at least three months. And the business manager at Mervyn's said, "Mrs. Auchard, PLEASE stop sending us money." I felt like Mrs. Stupid.

I'm still learning, and I make big boo-boos every week. But the road to recovery and self-sufficiency has been as filled with laughter, creativity, connection, and transformation as it has tears, self-doubt, and lonely nights. Now I'm doing so well that I sometimes feel guilty. But after suffering a loss, surviving and thriving are imperative for recovery and should be celebrated. I'm more than content. I'm eager to see what happens next.

Part 1: *He's Gone*

Blue Skies

My husband, Denny, had been undergoing aggressive chemotherapy for seven months. Sometimes he felt pretty good. He could drive, eat at a restaurant, and stay up for several hours doing easy jobs at his desk. But much of the time he was weak and tired. He couldn't be on his feet for long — ten minutes would have been a record. Because he was so weary, he often dozed in his recliner as I settled in my lounge chair beside him.

One day, our dog was asleep on my lap while Denny's eyes were closed in rest. His chin was down, his arms folded across his chest as usual. But I noticed that his lips were puckered as though giving someone a kiss. It was so amusing that I stared at him and wondered what he was dreaming.

Then I heard a thin little sound. It brought me to attention and caused the dog's ears to go erect. We both stared in disbelief as Denny slowly, but distinctly, whistled the first two lines of *Blue Skies*:

> *Blue skies, smilin' at me,*
> *Nothin' but blue skies do I see.*

When Denny's mouth relaxed, the tune faded. He returned to quiet slumber, but what a curious performance it had been! He was asleep yet awake — gone but not gone. And, in the midst of chemotherapy, he was dreaming of smiling blue skies.

Then I had a scary thought: "Lord, I hope he's not dreaming about heaven so soon, because I'm not ready."

While He Was Dying

I bought more sheets, more gowns, and foods that were easy to swallow to nourish him while he was dying. I set up fans and carefully arranged them to mask the heat that invaded the room. I bathed his arms, wiped his lips, and squeezed a dropper filled with water to wet his mouth, for I imagined him thirsty while he was dying.

I kissed his lips, stared at his face, smiled at him faintly, and patted his arm. I changed his bed. I washed the sheets, kept him clean, and fed our helpers the food from neighbors. But I forgot to eat, forgot to rest, forgot to pray, and forgot to cry while he was dying.

I was so tired, and he was so weak. He wanted to go, but I wished he could stay so I could say goodbye. I hadn't said it yet. I was afraid. "Goodbye" was too final and I wasn't quite ready.

I waited too long. He wanted to leave and went to sleep so he could die. He slept for hours, breathing peacefully. I finally did it — I whispered "goodbye," hoping he'd heard me. I stayed by his side as his breathing grew slower, and I counted the seconds between his breaths. It seemed so important to keep track of time. I don't know why — it was something to do.

One of our daughters held his hand. Her head bowed low, and she cried softly. We knew he was leaving; his breathing had changed. Slowly breathing, barely breathing, and then no breathing. Finally — dying.

Driving Denny

During our forty-nine years of marriage, Denny was rarely a passenger in our car. Wherever we went, he drove, and I rode along. It was that simple. No questions asked. A mutual assumption had been made by both of us so long ago that I had forgotten the reason. But this driving arrangement was about to change forever.

Denny's fast-growing cancer required such aggressive treatments that he was often too ill to drive. That's when I became his official chauffeur — and when I remembered the reason I never drove when he was the passenger. He was the king of back-seat drivers.

Though ill and weak, he found the strength to become my personal driver's education instructor. Many of his tips were helpful, but most of his comments were criticisms. His "instruction" never ended. Once I actually counted fourteen comments about my driving during one round trip to Kaiser Hospital. Lots of trips to Kaiser, lots of "helpful" tips, lots of stress headaches.

I protested — "Enough already!" — and put him on a ration of five criticisms per round-trip. My darling Denny tried, but it wasn't easy for him to keep his mouth shut. Out of the corner of my eye, I would notice his hand fly up to issue directions, but he'd catch himself and pretend to adjust his cap or scratch his head. He might start to use a cautionary tone, but instead substitute a fake little cough or pretend that he had forgotten whatever he was going to say. And so it went until he eventually returned to full-time monitoring of every mile I drove.

I tried the honest, up-front approach. "Honey, when I drive alone I have a lot of confidence, but when you're in the car I have none at all. My driving is growing worse. I'm anxious when you're my p-p-passenger [I started to cry right about here], and I dread these trips more than I can possibly tell you." The tears I shed were really big, and Denny felt terrible.

He felt so bad that he began to *compliment* my driving. He praised my ability to stay in the middle of my own lane, my parking skills, my confidence as I passed slow cars, and my overall driving improvement. It was like being patted on the head or patronized, so I never quite got out of my angry mode. I prayed a lot: "God, help Denny get off my back, or help me ignore him while I'm driving. I don't want to spend our precious time together being mad." We were in the car a lot, so I prayed a lot!

Denny got sicker as his cancer spread, but he still had a mission concerning my driving. He managed to sneak in a comment — or two, or three, or more — on every trip to the hospital, and I finally grew accustomed to it after almost ten months of treatment. Perhaps God had whispered to me, "Betty, get used to it. He doesn't have much time left."

Indeed, he didn't. Aggressive treatment was hurting him more than helping and it had to be discontinued. He was glad to be free of it, but he was visibly thinner, weaker, and more frail than ever before. During his last week of life, our family surrounded Denny, and someone was always at his side. When he grew too weak to speak, he would smile and make a kiss with his lips or pat someone's arm. He died gently, as we laid our hands on him and cried. We were grateful that his struggle was over, but we were also numb with grief and exhaustion.

The two weeks following Denny's death are a blur. It was a montage of paper signing, arrangements for private and public services, phone calls, out-of-state relatives, food appearing from nowhere, tears, hugging, and shared memories.

Once things finally settled down, the relatives were gone and so was the food. Thank-you notes were written. Wonderful, supportive letters arrived each day filled with memories of Denny, and it felt good to cry. But it was quiet and lonely. I had so many things to do, but I couldn't decide what to do first, so I did nothing.

One morning I received a call from the memorial park. "Mrs. Auchard, we have your husband's cremains ready for you." The container was small and wrapped neatly in brown paper. It was presented to me in a dark green, velour drawstring bag. I hugged it to my chest, then set it in the seat beside me — the passenger seat. I patted it gently and even considered protecting it with a seat belt.

Something occurred to me as I drove this container home. This was probably the only time in our forty-nine years of life together that Denny was my passenger and wouldn't be saying a word about my driving. I caressed the velour bag again and wiped away my tears so I could see where I was going — 'cuz you gotta stay alert when you're driving Denny.

Denny, Jim, and Me

It's quite possible that Denny and Jim died on the very same sheet, but I'll never know for sure. I do know that Jim spent his final days fading away on four of Denny's extra-long hospital linens because I shared them with him after Denny's death.

I met Jim in my first year as a high school art teacher when I was assigned to develop a photography program with this peppy guy. Jim was ten years younger than I and reminded me of a sandy-haired Peter Pan. On his days off he smoked and drank with the worst of them and made a party worth attending. I was young in spirit at forty-two, so we made a dynamite team. Together, we built the photography station cubicles by partitioning off work areas with plywood, equipping them with hand-me-down enlargers from the college, and hooking each one to a wall plug with long extension cords plugged into other long extension cords. Our handiwork was never inspected by anyone, and I now shudder to think how unsafe it might have been.

At the end of my first year of teaching, Jim and I were winding down for summer vacation. With school almost out for the year, we teachers were looking forward to a frisky end-of-year party at a local hot spot.

Jim asked, "Is Denny coming to the bash?"

"Nope, he has a meeting in Washington, DC."

"I'm glad because tonight, when the time is right, I need to talk to you about something important."

Jim's expression was unsettling, and all sorts of scenarios flashed through my mind. Mostly, I thought I might be the object of a workplace "crush" and that he planned to declare his deep affection for me. I was uneasy about the approaching evening and filled with dread and embarrassment.

That night, after a high old time with my colleagues, I had almost forgotten Jim's mention of our important conversation. But when we were finally alone in our booth, my best male friend leaned close to my face, looked straight into my eyes, and said, "Listen carefully. Don't react; just hear what I have to say."

"OK," I said. With an attentive expression and a hammering heart, I prepared myself for his amorous advances.

"I'm gay," he said. He didn't even blink.

I was too stunned to breathe, and it took a few seconds before I could speak. "But…what about…your girlfriend?"

"She's my good friend, and we've known each other for many years. There's nothing between us but friendship."

I didn't know if I was relieved or disappointed by this news. The fact that Jim was gay made me want to cry, but I had no idea why.

He ended with, "Betty, our friendship means a lot to me, and we're a great teaching team as well as best buddies. I would have LOVED having you for a mother."

I said good-bye to my permanently damaged ego and spent the rest of the evening learning about Jim's double life. He had been confused when he was young and, as a result, married at seventeen and divorced a year later. It took therapy before Jim eventually accepted that he was a normal homosexual man. So on weekends, he and his life partner shared a home in San Francisco, and during the week, he lived in a co-owned duplex with his long-time lady friend in the city where he taught art.

During our many years of teaching together, Jim became my best friend. We worked closely on school projects because we shared the same level of creative energy. The kids really liked us, and if one was asked to sponsor a dance, the other was expected to share the job. When Jim's students invited him to a midnight showing of the *Rocky Horror Picture Show*, they added, "Bring Mrs. Auchard along because we want to watch her face during the toast-throwing scene." The kids provided me with a "kit," which included the essential paraphernalia brought to each show by every savvy member of the audience. It was an outrageous night as we booed the villain, viewed sex scenes as shadow pictures, and watched costumed actors dance on the stage alongside the actors on the screen. We yelled a lot and waved flashlights in the air. And the kids kept stretching to get a glimpse of my face every time they heard me scream, "Oh, my God, I can't BELIEVE this movie!" They loved the fact that they were baptizing me into their world with a nonschool activity, and I loved it as much as they did — maybe more.

Jim and I spent a great deal of time going to school functions, and it sometimes ruffled Denny's feathers. He said, "You seem to have more fun with Jim than with me." Although Jim was a playful guy and full of energy, he was never competition for my Denny. And although Denny envied the camaraderie I shared with Jim, my husband liked him as much as I did. Denny and I were guests in Jim's San Francisco home many times. He and his partner were marvelous hosts, and Jim was a wonderful cook. He even had a dream of running a small, elite catering business after retiring. Whenever Denny was gone during the summer, I was invited to spend a weekend or two with the guys. I loved it because they treated me like royalty, taking me to popular diners for unusual edibles.

"What is that?" I asked when Jim spread a dark mixture on bits of French bread.

"Steak tartare. Do you want a taste?"

"Sure." I gave my full attention to the culinary experience. "Wow. This is interesting!"

Jim laughed when he said, "Betty, you're so much fun to take places."

"Really?"

"You're impressed with everything, just like a country bumpkin in the big city." The name stuck, and Jim often referred to me as "Country Bumpkin," even when we weren't in San Francisco.

Eventually I retired from teaching, though Jim was too young for retirement. We stayed in close touch for many years, but gradually drifted apart. On rare occasions we talked on the phone when there was special news to exchange, and we always traded Christmas cards.

But Jim showed up one day when I most needed him. As I was leaving the hospital where Denny had been admitted, I realized that Jim did not know of Denny's grave condition. I had just formed the thought that I must call Jim in the morning when I looked up to see him walking toward me. I was shocked. He was so happy to see me that he hugged me tight and asked, "What in the world brings you to the hospital this late?"

Phrases spilled in all directions as I told Jim that I had just been thinking about him and then he appeared. I flung words at him that I hoped made sense as I hammered out the details of Denny's illness. I had no tears because

I was numb from the bad news of Denny's diagnosis and stunned by Jim's appearance. He had materialized like magic.

I got a grip on myself enough to say, "What a shock to see you here."

We talked in the parking lot for an hour amidst cars coming and going when I realized that it was growing dark. Jim said, "I need to get inside and get some blood tests taken, but we've got to stay in touch."

Sadly, Jim's blood tests led to other tests that revealed that he, too, had lung cancer. The only difference was that Jim was a smoker and his type of cancer was treatable.

Denny and Jim became cancer buddies. They talked on the phone frequently, comparing symptoms and treatments. We thought Jim had a good chance of recovering but that Denny did not, though he refused to accept that probability. My husband believed that he could beat the disease until the very end when his approaching death was inevitable. Only then did he concede.

After Denny's death, Jim and I stayed in touch. I visited him even after he became gravely ill and was limited to spending his final days in a hospital bed at home. It was then that I suggested he use Denny's sheets instead of buying new ones. Sometimes when I was Jim's visitor, he was so weak that he slept through my stay. I spent the time talking with his partner about the experience of being a caregiver for someone we loved. Eventually, Jim faded away and died on the same sheets on which Denny had died. After his partner returned the carefully folded linens to me, I shared them with no one else, but I did use them myself.

Two important men in my life may have died on the same panel of percale. When I pondered that possibility, my eyes stung as they do now while writing about those wonderful guys. It also gives me a mysterious sense of peace that Denny and Jim might be watching over me and feeling proud of how I'm doing. I wonder if they talk about me now that they're gone? And what might they be saying? When Jim reads this account of the night that he told me he was gay instead of telling me that he had fallen crazy in love with me, will he laugh? Will Denny confess to Jim that he was a tad jealous of our close friendship? Maybe someday they'll tell me.

Apple Butter for Denny

Core and slice a lot of apples, about two paper grocery bags half full, but don't peel them. In a large, heavy pot, add a small amount of water to the sliced apples and cook on low heat until soft. Watch and stir. Add a bit more water, if needed. Press through a sieve or food mill to remove the skins. It should yield eight cups. If you leave it this way, you'll have applesauce.

To make apple butter, take the eight cups of pulp, one-half cup of vinegar, four cups of brown sugar, two teaspoons of ground cinnamon, and mix well. Return to the heavy pot and cook on low heat, stirring to prevent burning. It will take a long time.

While waiting, write a poem, a story, or both. Once the mixture stays in a smooth mass when a little is cooled on a saucer, you have apple butter. It should make three pints. Seal in sterilized jars, or just spread on good bread and eat, which is what Denny used to do when I made my mother's recipe for him with fruit from our neighbor's tree.

My neighbor gave me two bags of apples today, as she does every year, so I made Denny's apple butter. He barely tolerated my mother, but he found her recipe irresistible. I'm not fond of apple butter — too mooshy — but Denny loved it, so I made it for him even though he's not here. Cancer took him seven weeks ago. A harsh word, "cancer." Apple butter isn't harsh; it's smooth and sweet, so I made it to feel closer to Denny.

I knew for months that he would die, but it didn't prepare me for living without him. I had no idea it would be so hard! But you can't rush through grief as though it were housework. Someday I'll think of Denny and smile instead of crying. I hope that's true — I miss him so much. His apple butter tastes better than I remember. He would have loved it, and I may learn to love it, too. But not as much as I loved Denny.

Putting My Grief on the Line

I should read my bereavement books during the daytime instead of at night. At night, I dissolve into tears and fall asleep too soon. Would I do the same during the day? I'll never know because I can't make myself sit down with a book when the sun is shining. That's when my grief feels more controlled, even though I'm so preoccupied that I've almost had accidents while driving. I appear normal as I do laundry or pay the bills. But I'm really grinding out memories, which results in using no laundry soap or paying more money than I owe on bills.

So I save reflecting for nighttime. After crawling into bed, I pick up my book and fine-tip pen from the nightstand, and then open to where I left off the night before. After a few pages, I feel compelled to add my two cents in the margins.

Last week I read, "Many survivors have unresolved issues with the deceased." Alongside that sentence I wrote, "Oh, yes." Since I had more to say,

I said it on the blank pages at the back of the book in very small handwriting. I wept as I crammed words from my heart into a one-inch space. That's the way it usually goes until, sooner or later, I use up my tears for the night. I mark my place in the book, turn out the light, and try to go to sleep. But it doesn't always work. Sometimes I lie there and ponder until a new thought occurs to me — and I turn on the light to write more.

Whenever I feel I must write things down, I grab whatever's handy — a receipt, a paper napkin, or the back of a used envelope. I don't remember what I wrote about once it's written. I don't even know where I've put those bits of paper filled with feelings that had to be preserved. But it's not important that I save the words. It's the act of putting my grief on the line that keeps Denny here a little longer.

Negotiations Have Ended

After several months of being a widow, I had regained a fragment of my stability. I still cried when I felt like it, but I was learning to stay afloat. Three times in a row I paid the bills on time, and I did all I could to follow Denny's master budget plan. But I wanted to do more than just follow the leader, so, feeling plucky, I decided to make some changes on my own. The things around me that we had shared for almost forty-nine years were a constant, painful reminder that he was gone. Meeting widowhood head-on, I started replacing our belongings.

The first thing to go was our massive, dark walnut bedroom furniture. Alone, I was lost on that king-sized mattress. My daughter and her husband, who lived with an odd assortment of fixtures, took all six pieces. It was their first bedroom set, and they were thrilled. The room where I had slept with Denny for decades was now empty. I moved into the computer room, sleeping on a day bed at night and shopping each day for a set of my own. After many weeks of searching, I found a charming Shaker set that I longed for. And it was on sale! I put strips of masking tape on the floor and walls of the bedroom, pretending it was three-dimensional. It fit, so I ordered every piece and left town for two weeks on my first trip without Denny.

While I was watching two live shows a day in Branson, Missouri, my children were at home painting the master bedroom and bath with my all-time, favorite noncolor, Kelly Moore Navajo white. The furniture arrived while I was away, and my family set all six pieces in their designated places. When I returned to my new nest, with the bed freshly made and nothing yet on the walls, I felt that I had taken the first steps in starting my life over.

That night, while flossing my teeth in the newly painted bathroom, I noticed the gray front tooth that had always bugged me despite the fact that Denny never noticed it. Even my eighty-year-old mother, who had cataracts, had asked, "Is your front tooth kinda gray or are my eyes gettin' worse?"

Denny insisted, "I never even notice that dark tooth, honey. Forget about it."

But I never did, and I wanted that ugly tooth out of my face. With little thought to the master budget plan, I made an appointment the next day to have my four front teeth capped. Then, I pondered what I might do next.

There were many things on our master list, but Denny and I could never agree on what should come first, so our life-improvement projects often bogged down during negotiations. I wanted double-pane windows; he wanted new carpets. I wanted new copper pipes; he wanted a new car. I wanted a cell phone, e-mail service, and an ATM card; but he declared, "Honey, that stuff isn't necessary." Just thinking about what I could do on my own brightened my mood significantly. I could do what I wanted without negotiating.

Without negotiating.

The words shot through my heart and ripped it open. While staring at the gray front tooth that I was about to replace, I wept because negotiations had ended — *forever.*

The Mark on the Rug

There is a mark on the rug where his chest of drawers once stood. It is a gentle reminder that it was once his side of the bedroom, the neater side, where nothing ever changed. There were only a few items, always in the same place, and never any dust there — ever. No piles of books, catalogues, and other things to be put away later, sometime, maybe. That kind of clutter was on my side — on top of my dresser.

"You need to clean that up sometime, honey," he said to me gently, but often. I just left it, cleaning only when guests might be coming upstairs. There was never a doubt which side of the room was mine.

His chest of drawers once held his clothes, his keys, his wallet, and the badges he earned during his youth (including one for speed typing). An old cigar box protected insignias from his military service. The bottom drawer was filled with stiff terrycloth letters he earned for college athletics.

Denny still tried to stay physically fit — for an old guy — and usually woke before I did, starting his morning stretches right on the bed as he lay beside me. As he stretched his leg over, up, and out, it flew across his own body and then across mine. He stretched it out as far as he could, brought it back, and then stretched his other leg over my body, whopping me with it as I lay still under the covers.

After a few leg whops, he jumped out of bed and tucked in his sheets, straightened the blanket, fluffed his pillow, and smoothed the bedspread on his side of the bed — all while I was still in it, barely awake. It restricted my movement and turned me into a living mummy. This entire routine bounced me awake before I was ready. It was his way of saying, "It's time to rise and shine, Betty." I usually did rise, but I never did shine.

I reflect on these memories as I gaze at the impression in the carpet where his furniture once rested. The trinkets have gone to our boys, and the clothes have been given away. The dresser now makes its mark in another house, on another rug. When this carpet is torn out and tossed, the impression will leave with it. The ghost mark on the rug will go to the dump. What a sorry place for memories to be buried — at the dump! I can't bear to think of it. What marks will be left then to remind me that we once shared this room?

Never Stop Moving

Since Denny died four and a half months ago, I've had my ups and downs. Emotionally, I've lived a lifetime. I've learned a lot, laughed a lot, cried a lot, and cooked very little. Physically, I'm weighed down with jobs I've never done before. There is so much to do that I'm afraid to pause. I'm overwhelmed and completely behind on everything. My memory has become terrible and my tongue feels swollen, which makes me lisp, but I can't worry about a fat tongue. Sometimes, I wonder if I'll ever sew or cook again, or if I'll ever gain control of all these new responsibilities. Last week I forgot to put out the garbage, and I've been moping about it ever since. I make lists of things I must not forget, and then I can't find the lists. I'm tired most of the time.

Tonight, I almost declined my fifteen-year-old granddaughter's invitation to watch her ballet class. She was one of three students who would practice with their teacher for two hours. Two hours? Could I afford this kind of time? I needed to pay bills and balance the checkbook!

But off I went to a chilly studio to settle into a hard chair for an evening of student ballet. Little did I know that I was about to be entranced. The vivacious, young instructor was a joy to watch as she demonstrated ballet steps and chirped out never-ending instructions.

"Sue-sue, passay, eelawnjay, pleeay" is what it sounded like. I didn't know what the lovely French sounds meant, but the dancers apparently did, as they responded to the instructions in unison. The music was contagious, and the graceful movements of the students were exciting to watch. The teacher kept up her pace, encouraging the girls with, "Never stop moving. Keep your head up, your back straight, and your hands in the ready position! You're getting better at this, but you're turning purple. Breathe, breathe, don't forget to breathe!" I followed her instructions, obediently breathing deeply. It felt great! Had I forgotten how to breathe?

The students responded to the message of the music and encouragement of their teacher — and so did I! I heard, "Don't give up! Stay with the music! Never stop moving!" I felt like dancing, too.

Then she urged, "Now rest a bit, stretch a bit, get a drink of water. How's everybody doing? Are you ready to go again?"

"Yes, yes!" I wanted to shout! "I'll never stop moving! I'll stay with the music! I'm ready to go again!" I wasn't tired anymore, and I felt good. I knew I'd be able to keep my home and life in order, and I knew I would get better at it, too. With practice I would improve — just like the other dancers.

May Memories

The rose garden blossoms with bits of color. It's always like this in May — on the verge of breathtaking. When the garden was this beautiful a year ago, Denny was beginning his gradual descent into a place of his own where we couldn't follow. I see our garden in all its glory and my thoughts drift back to those difficult days. Then, my sadness becomes more intense than ever. Everything brings tears to my eyes.

I dread the sneaky reflections that may creep up on me next month, the month of June. But, most of all, I fear July, when he left us forever. My friend Jean said to me, "Memories of suffering grow dim and sweet remembrance will come to soften the pain of loss." I must believe that she's right, for I dread these memories of Denny's final days.

Tears Welling

I am flying to an annual conference of counselor educators to accept an award in Denny's memory — and it's happening again. It starts with my thoughts, then tightens my throat, stings my nose like needles, and turns my eyes to water.

It's not the same as crying, which is gently explosive. Crying is much harder to conceal. This I call "tears welling," and it sneaks up on me. I know what causes it — sad, reflective feelings. If only I could control them in public places. Sometimes I can. For example, if it happens while waiting in a grocery store line, I can interrupt the blues by taking slow, deep breaths so my eyes don't water. Sucking air into my lungs with purpose gives me something else to do — a distraction that gets my mind off of melancholy.

It also keeps me from scaring other people who might think I'm grieving over the high cost of food or the long wait in line. However, if I linger on the memories a moment too long, there I am with tears hanging out of my eyes while trying to pay the grocery bill. In that event, I attempt to avoid eye contact by examining the chewing gum labels by the cash register.

If my tears get away from me, I disguise them by passing them off as eye drops. I whip out my plastic bottle, tip my head way back, and squeeze a little into each eye. It's the kind of thing that happens in a grocery store. People are uncomfortable when they see someone weeping in public, but no one ever questions eye drops dribbling down a person's cheeks. I wouldn't go anywhere without them. I also carry a handkerchief in case the dam *really* breaks.

Now, don't think I'm afraid to cry. I'm not. I just don't like bursting into tears at the sight of a jar of Postum on the grocery shelf. When I'm at home and I become downhearted, I make no attempt to stop what happens next. It's welcome. It feels good, even though it's painful. It's what my mother used to call a "good hurt."

My mother, who never graduated from high school, was proud of Denny. Even though his family was poorer than ours, he put himself through college and eventually became a university professor. As a professor, my husband belonged to many professional organizations with names that reduced to acronyms. He attended meetings all over the country. I knew he was doing important work that helped others, but I had no idea he was one of the founders of an organization called ACAF. And now, after all these years, he is being honored because of his contribution to the field of counseling.

Over twenty years ago, I didn't comprehend the scope of Denny's professional involvement. I was too busy chauffeuring our four children everywhere while finishing my college degree. I wish I could have appreciated his work while he was doing it.

How would Denny feel if he could know where I am going today? I think he would be deeply moved by this gesture from his colleagues.

It's happening again — feeling weepy. I'm alone in this row, so I'll turn my head to the window and pretend to be studying the ocean. Breathe, breathe. Don't forget to breathe.

Oh, to heck with it. The tears welling can just run down my cheeks this time. It's only a trickle, but it sure . . . hurts . . . good.

Hiding the Truth

For several months after Denny's death, I did everything in my power to keep strange men from knowing that I was a brand new widow. The façade wasn't easy when I had men coming to clean the furnace or to give me estimates for repairing the sprinkler system. To make it appear as though I had a husband and grown sons who lived here, I said things like, "I'm the one who gets the bids while the 'guys' are at work."

I desperately needed new shower doors in two bathrooms and had gotten a recommendation from a general contractor in the neighborhood. I checked out the showroom display, found the doors I liked, ordered them, and scheduled a day for installation. To leave the strong impression that I did *not* live alone, I told the salesman that I would save money by having one of my sons or my husband clean the old sealer from the surface of the shower stalls.

I was confident I could do the job myself, but it was more labor intensive than I'd expected. My hands ached from the effort, and I soon begrudged the measly $60 I'd saved. But it was worth it to leave the impression that I lived in the house with men who protected me.

Before "shower door installation day" arrived, I placed extra stuff around both bathrooms. I put several toothbrushes in the holders, hung more towels on the racks, and set out cologne and shavers that had belonged to Denny. Since one of the bathrooms opened onto my bedroom, I positioned Denny's slippers and housecoat near the bed and placed a football trophy on top of the dresser. With all that junk around it did not appear that I lived alone — no siree! That was the kind of clutter that guys made.

When the installer arrived, he got right to work without appearing to notice any of my stage props. But he said, "Your family did a good job preparing this surface for the new caulking. It's way better than I would have done." I felt so proud that I almost took a bow to thank him and tell him how hard I'd worked — but I stopped myself just in time.

After he had installed both doors, he cleaned up his mess, put his tools away, and handed me the bill. I paid him, I thanked him, and he left. It was that simple. I was so relieved that I let out an audible sigh as soon as he was gone. Then I began to remove the carefully placed objects I'd used to fool the stranger who had occupied my house for one short hour. That's when I noticed my side of the bed.

It was quite obvious that only one person had slept there. The other side of the bed was neat and unruffled. That pillow was plump and smooth. The covers were still tucked in. The entire scene almost shouted, "Only one person sleeps in this bed, and she is a defenseless woman who lives here alone and can be ravaged at knife-point at any time of the day or night."

I didn't know whether to laugh out loud or be afraid for my next night alone. So I did neither. I got my mind off the subject by taking a shower and noticing how transparent the new shower doors were. It meant that an intruder could see me naked. But it also meant that I could see him coming, which would give me time to grab a bar of soap and throw it at him with one hand while dialing 911 with the other — IF I remembered to take the telephone into the shower.

My Request

The closer I got to the first anniversary of Denny's death on July ninth, the sadder and more melancholy I became. Filled with anxiety, I finally sought help from a counseling group. During a bereavement workshop we were given the following line to finish: "If this were my last summer on earth, I would like …" I wrote my assignment in the form of a letter.

Denny,

Hon, if this were my last summer on earth, I would hope that you could send me a message and say that you're proud of how I'm doing. I need your approval about decisions I've made. I want to know if you trust my judgment and my ability to carry on without you at my side. I wish I trusted myself, but there's a shadow hanging over me that has stolen my confidence. Please come to me in a dream and tell me honestly that you feel I've done well. I could do with some validation to continue this widow journey. I probably haven't dreamed of you because I dread your reaction to the way I'm running things around here. Please give me a sign. I long to hear you say, "Good job, Betty! I'm proud of you! I knew you could do it!"

❋ ❋ ❋

Not 'til It's Finished

I never used our computer when my husband was alive. If I wanted something written, I dictated and he typed. Learning technology on my own was a chore. It took almost six months before I could write a story with the keyboard instead of with pen and paper. But I finally got the hang of it, and now I call my grandkids for help only once a week instead of daily.

One day, I was determined to explore all the files that Denny had in our computer. It was a daunting task, like wandering into a warehouse crammed with countless rooms. Of course, I got lost. I couldn't find my way home or repeat my steps. I was in an unfamiliar place when I opened a screen full of manila folders labeled with amputated words that meant nothing to me. I finally clicked on a file that revealed a watercolor leaf print of mine with the message, "Betty is a wonderful person."

"Oh, my goodness!" I sat stunned, practically immobilized. Then tears exploded from my eyes, and I slumped in my computer chair and bawled. Denny took pleasure in making all kinds of cards with messages, but he had never shown me that one before. I eventually pulled myself together and clicked on another file.

"HI, BETTY."

Another greeting thrust Denny into the room, and his presence was so real that I felt I could have touched him. I burst into tears again at the sight of a cartoon pilot wearing a helmet and goggles, with a scarf around his neck that trailed behind him. Inside the cartoon balloon over the pilot's head was Denny's message.

Then I remembered what the images were all about. Denny had been designing a business card for me as a surprise. "The image I like best," he had said two years ago, "is the watercolor maple leaf I scanned from one of your travel journals." These images were the first rough drafts of his design ideas.

At the time, I could hardly wait for him to create the final design, but he wouldn't let me see it until it was done.

"Please show it to me, hon."

"Not 'til it's finished."

He never did finish my business cards because cancer got in the way. But there was something wonderful about stumbling across those unexpected messages from Denny. Maybe my surprise was finished after all.

Emotions: The First Year

Denny died a little over a year ago, and my process of recovering from grief has been full of surprises. Sometimes I'm up, sometimes I'm down, and sometimes I'm in the middle. It's never a smooth, straight line.

The earlier months were painful and dark, but sometimes light and hopeful. It felt as good to cry as to laugh, and I did my share of both. These opposing feelings leveled out to periods of normalcy that never lasted more than a few weeks. The dark and gloomy days of March, with their heavy rains and lack of sunshine, had a disastrous effect on my spirits. Being housebound because of the weather pulled me even lower than I thought I could go. During that time I didn't accomplish much of anything. When the rain stopped and the sun came out, the world looked much brighter.

My up-and-down moods occurred many times before I felt stable again. In fact, I thought I was fully recovered from the loss of my husband. I was certain of it and was caught by surprise when the blues snuck up on me again. Each day I felt more apprehensive, and I finally had to seek help from my support system: family, friends, and eventually, my counselor. Miraculously, I came through all of it much better than I'd expected.

In fact, I felt surprisingly blissful and almost euphoric — an unusual emotional high. I felt so much excitement about embracing the future that one night, as I lay in bed reflecting on my emotional stamina, I wept tears of joy. I was happy and grateful. I began to feel like a normal, recovered person. It was wonderful!

But when I least expected it, old, resentful thoughts crept into my consciousness, dredging up unresolved issues between Denny and me. Things that I thought were history lined themselves up in my memory for roll call. There was the time he didn't think the dog needed a vet to help deliver her pups — even though she was taking so long. And when he grumbled about my increased weight by saying, "Look at you. You've gained ten pounds." Another time, he bought a TV surround sound system for "us" instead of a garden mulcher for me and said, "More people can enjoy an upgraded sound system than a thing that grinds up sticks and leaves."

It's likely that these issues would *never* have been resolved, even if he'd lived another seventy-two years. And the worst part was that they still made me mad! Was it normal to feel resentment towards a loved one so long after his death? I didn't want to feel that way, but I couldn't move on until I put it behind me. What bothered me most was that the anger had interrupted my wonderful forward movement.

Gradually, the hostile feelings toward Denny simply wore off. Maybe they resolved themselves without my being consciously aware of it. A sense of peace settled tenuously around me. I knew the roller coaster of emotions I'd experienced during that first year would continue for a while, although not as frequently and with less intensity. Someday, I would feel normal again. I was almost sure of it.

Dry Eyes

I came across some notes that I'd scribbled in a small tablet three months ago. The notes described the physical sensation and slight pain I experienced whenever tears came. It happened so often that I became familiar with the path it traveled to reach my eyes. Tears were my constant companion, so I wrote about them in a piece called "Tears Welling."

When I read this piece now, I can barely remember the "good hurt." At that time, I was convinced that for the rest of my life the slightest memory of Denny would make my eyes water. But, it isn't so. I think of him daily, and my eyes are dry.

Denny has been gone for one year, and the pain is gradually lifting from my heart. I'm involved with the rest of the world again and am less reflective than I was six months ago. I want to embrace my life, for I sense that exciting things are waiting to happen to me in a new life without so much weeping.

I know that I have the capacity for happiness without Denny beside me. I like that feeling, but I'm not yet ready to say good-bye.

Part 2: *Reflecting*

Wilma Gets Married

*W*ilma, my college girlfriend, was engaged to be married. I had never been friends with a bride-to-be and found it *quite* educational. And I wasn't the only one; five of us often huddled in her dorm room, spellbound with conversations about premarital bliss. Among those in our inner circle, she was the oldest. I was the youngest and thrilled to be included in the late night girlie chats in her dormitory room. We marveled at all that happens before a wife-to-be takes those final steps to the altar.

One night as we crowded around the edges of her bed, leaning on our elbows, she took her usual lotus-legged position with her hands outstretched, palms up, and announced, "Today . . . I got fitted for a diaphragm." She knew how to get our attention and she knew more about sex than we did, so we were riveted to every word she spoke.

"And the doctor said that he may have to . . . cut my hymen."

Oh, was she good — we gasped in unison.

"Cut it — why?" I was brave enough to ask.

"Because it's so thick that on my wedding night, it could be a painful experience." (We all knew that "it" meant having sex for the first time.)

I sucked in my breath when I heard THAT line, and one of the older girls said, "Thank goodness mine is already broken."

"What have you been *doing?*" someone asked.

"It happened when I was eleven, playing on a fire hydrant. I slipped and fell spread-eagle right on top of the lid."

Wilma, sensing that she might lose her audience, said, "Well I wasn't that lucky. I have an appointment with a doctor."

"Are you actually going to do that?" I asked.

"I guess so. But I need to do it real soon so it'll be healed before the wedding."

I suppressed a shudder and wondered what it was like to have tissue "down there" stretched out by a fire hydrant or a guy — or cut by a doctor.

The next night we gathered in Wilma's room to hear another prenuptial bedtime story. But it wasn't as scintillating as the night before. Wilma hadn't prepared a good opening and hesitated with her lips parted as if trying to catch words in the air. We were uncomfortable with no sound coming from our leader, but she finally broke the silence.

"Today . . . I got cold feet."

I imagined a cartoon balloon above our heads with "uh-oh" written in it.

"I went to the mailbox to drop off my wedding invitations, raised the lid, put them into the opening . . . and couldn't let go of them. I said out loud, 'What am I doing?'"

"Don't you love him?" the fire hydrant girl asked.

"Sure, I love him a whole bunch, but it bothers me that his IQ is lower than mine."

I made a mental note to check the IQ of any potential husband.

"What did you finally decide?" someone asked.

"Well, I really do love him — so I mailed the invitations."

Wilma mailed all 100 envelopes, and the wedding proceeded as planned — with me as the wedding singer. It was a festive event, and I never sang better. At *almost nineteen*, wearing a floor-length silk dress and high-heeled shoes, I felt like an adult.

Over three decades later, after their three children were grown, Wilma and her husband went their separate ways. But if she hadn't mailed the wedding invitations that day, I would never have met their best man, the man I married four and a half months later. He passed the IQ test and, best of all, I was crazy about him.

The Guy in the Middle

The summer of 1949, I was eighteen and had just finished my first year of college. My summer job at an upscale country restaurant, the meeting place of local celebrities, required that I dress in high heels and mature clothes. I slept on tight knots of pin curls every night and lowered my skirt hem to three inches above the ankle, which was the current "new look." I was hot to trot.

Guys had finally begun to notice me during my freshman year of college because I had blossomed in more ways than one. I cut off my long braids, which made me look more modern. I wasn't shy anymore, and my confidence showed. There were more available men on our campus than I had ever seen in my life. The war had ended, and many young men had returned to college after serving in the military. Three former sailors worked in the restaurant with me. Each time I flirted with one of those guys, I thought to myself, "Hubba-hubba. He's goin' on MY summer schedule."

Everything would have been perfect if only I hadn't promised my college girlfriend that I would sing at her wedding in June. When she had asked two months earlier, I replied as though I'd spent my whole life preparing for that very moment.

"I would just LOVE to sing at your wedding," I gushed.

But two months had passed, and I had changed my mind. I had plans for the summer, and that agreement to be a wedding singer wasn't written in blood. I tried to back out.

She almost wept and whimpered, "How could you let me down at the last minute, unless you needed SURGERY or something?"

I wished I'd thought of that before calling her. But I was determined not to sing.

"I live so far away from you," I whined. "How am I going to get there?"

"I'll send my fiancé to give you a ride." She was quick.

I pondered how important her friendship was to me and considered getting pushy. Finally, I gave in and resigned myself to the inevitable.

"OK. I'll sing. Now, when is your wedding?"

I could almost feel heat through the phone when she said in a calm, but simmering, tone, "You've got two weeks to practice!"

With no enthusiasm whatsoever, I started warming up my voice with scales and "la-las," but I desperately wanted to get her wedding behind me. Summer fun was beckoning, and I wanted a head start with the popular oil and iodine formula that produced a quick tan.

The night of the rehearsal, the groom-to-be drove all the way from Denver to pick me up. I was grateful that my job meant wearing nice clothes, because a rehearsal dinner at the Country Club followed the wedding practice.

As we approached the church, I saw three handsome young men standing outside the door with arms folded across their manly chests like sentinels. I held my breath. Those weren't boys; they were men.

I momentarily forgot about my cute college waiters.

The groom broke my trance and said, "Betty, I want you to meet my roommates who are in the wedding party. They're from York College."

I felt suddenly self-conscious and ashamed that I had complained about living so far away. Those three men had come all the way from the East Coast to take part in the wedding. They must have been very close friends of the groom.

As we approached the handsome trio, the groom said, "Fellas, this is Betty, the wedding singer."

I smiled easily and said, "Hi, Glenn." (What a tall guy.) "Hi, Denny." (I'll take him!) "Hi, Harvey." (Whoa, another tall one.)

But I had eyes only for the guy in the middle — whom the groom introduced as the best man. He was definitely the best man I had ever seen — criminally handsome with black wavy hair, warm, brown eyes, and a smile so heartfelt that it burned a hole in my chest.

His stunning good looks were the first thing that got my attention, but his gracious, unpretentious manner finished me off. Denny didn't display the cocky self-confidence common in gorgeous guys. He was authentically nice, and he was so attentive during our first, brief conversation, that I suspected he felt the same about me. I was suddenly addled.

Because I was so nervous, I practiced singing "The Lord's Prayer" and "Ave Maria" with great difficulty. While I was warming up my voice, Denny slipped into the sanctuary where he was the only one in the pews. His full attention made it seem that I was auditioning for something. I wanted a callback so I tried to sing my very best in case it was true.

I couldn't stop thinking about him and decided to "accidentally" run into him. In between vocals I pretended to be thirsty and, in my stocking feet, went in search of water. He must have had the same idea because we met at the drinking fountain.

He said, "Hello, again. You look shorter."

"I sing my best without high heels."

"Most people sing their best in the shower." He was corny — how sweet!

I bent to get a drink, and Denny leaned forward to turn the faucet. My heart was pounding and I hoped that my hair looked nice from his angle. As he turned the knob, the drinking fountain sprayed my face and hair like a fire-hose and almost blew off my eyebrows. My bosom was drenched. Denny was horrified. He desperately searched his pockets for a handkerchief. I mopped my face and patted the stringy strands of wet hair falling onto my forehead. I barely patted the wet fabric over my breasts, aware that I was bringing too much attention to them. He was watching every move. What a mess he'd made of me! But getting drenched certainly broke the ice.

When the rehearsal dinner was over, the groom and best man drove me home in Denny's blue 1947 Dodge coupe. Denny allowed the groom to be the driver while I sat squished in the middle, pressed tight against Denny's hip. He rode in the passenger seat with his elbow hanging out the open window, eyes darting left and right while monitoring all traffic. He gave directions frequently and grimaced more than once. Denny finally said with some urgency, "Let's stop for a piece of pie."

"Sure thing," said the groom, and he turned sharply across the lane in front of oncoming traffic, causing Denny to rise up off the car seat and yell, "WHOA-WHOA-WHOA! BOY, THAT WAS A CLOSE ONE!"

After we finished our pie á la modes and cherry Cokes, Denny studied the bill and checked the math before paying it. Then he turned to the groom and said, "I'll drive."

During the long drive to my house, I had a chance to review all that I'd learned about Denny. While in the diner, I found out that he was older than the other guys, and had beautiful teeth and a great smile that made him even more desirable than he already was. He was gentle in manner, only slightly humorous and curiously cautious. As we talked, I also learned that he taught physics and mathematics at York College. Wow! He was definitely out of my league, and I knew it. But it was OK. Once he returned to New York I could get back to my sun-tanning schedule, my waiters, and the rest of my summer.

But I felt strangely melancholy. That night I said to Mom as she read the newspaper, "The best man in the wedding took me out for pie on the way home. He's really nice but he's from out of state, fussy about his car, and picky about the check."

"Oh, one of those types, huh?" said Mom.

"Yeah, and besides that, he's too old for me."

"How do you know?"

"Well, he's a gray-haired professor from New York."

"Oh, what a dirty rotten shame." Mom actually put down the *Denver Post* to say that.

I couldn't have been more dejected if I'd just discovered that Denny was an ex-convict. My shoulders slumped and I chewed on a hangnail.

What I didn't know about Denny was that he was only twenty-three and prematurely gray. He was not a professor from New York on the East Coast, but the youngest teacher at a small church college in York, Nebraska. I also had no way of knowing that by the end of my friend's wedding the next day, nothing in my life would ever be the same.

The summer of 1949 was going to be more eventful than I could ever have imagined.

Our "Courtship"

Denny was a good-looking, twenty-three-year-old stranger from out of town, and I was bobby soxer who had plans for the summer. But we were smitten the moment we met, he asked me out the next evening, and we dated the rest of the summer.

With Denny in summer school fifty miles away, weekends were the only time we saw each other We danced every week at Elitch Gardens, where we also rode on the roller coaster with our cheeks pushed flat against our faces. We rowed a rented boat in the City Park Lake. We dined in nice restaurants and ordered exotic deserts drenched with wine sauce — even though we didn't like it — because it seemed elegant.

And we learned about each other. I learned that his brother had been lost in the submarine service during the war. He learned that my parents had been married and divorced from each other three times. He grew up poor and so did I, so we compared "poor" stories. We played tennis and softball, and we necked — a lot; I tried kissing with my eyes open for the first time. Our romance progressed, Denny's schoolwork fell behind as we fell more in love, and quite soon we spoke of marriage.

My father was happy I had found my life partner, but my mother was not. She reminded me that our church disapproved of "mixed marriages." Denny may have been a preacher's kid, but he belonged to a church that did not have reserved seats in heaven, as ours did.

My mother, brother, sister, and I were new converts to our church, but my dad resisted a tithe or allegiance to anything but the Union. He witnessed our confirmation as new church members, but held to his views. "I've gotta lotta flaws," Dad said. "But joinin' a church ain't one of 'em." Dad was immune to my mother's influence. I was not.

Here I was, a recent convert, wanting to marry an "outsider." My mother began holding her breath, which would eventually bring on a panic attack. She scheduled a meeting with our reverend and he said to me, "Betty, if you expect to go to heaven, you must adhere to our beliefs." Well, what new convert doesn't want to go to heaven? I agreed, and my mother exhaled.

I was easily swayed and left our first meeting with a mission, which was to convert Denny, and I had the rest of the summer to do it. I armed myself with a catechism, and Denny, who suspected something was up, came to our next date with a Bible. We spent hours trying to find a loophole that would allow us to marry, when we could have been necking instead.

The summer was almost gone, nothing was resolved regarding our future, and my mother was breathless most of time, so she scheduled another meeting with the Reverend. This time, he said bluntly, "Betty, it is God's will that you give him up."

I was confused and dizzy from swaying back and forth between my faith and my love for Denny. During each weekend with him, I wanted us to spend our lives together. But after each meeting with the Reverend and my mother, I was convinced it was a sin to marry an outsider. My heart was broken, but I was afraid to mess with God. So, I agreed to give Denny up, and the color returned to my mother's cheeks.

Denny had no idea I was about to dump him. He was feeling pretty glum himself as he dropped to a "C" in one of his classes. It didn't help that he received the lowered grade and a "Dear John" letter at the same time. My letter explained in neat handwriting that I must give him up for good, because it was God's will. I didn't like God that summer, but I was only eighteen, and that's when I thought God was a man. Denny said it hurt even more that I had written such bad news on a postcard with scenic views of Denver. His heart fell to the ground. He'd let his grades slip for nothing!

Denny and I were miserable. So God sent two guardian angels to help reconcile our differences — the good friends at whose wedding Denny and I had met two months earlier. Our angels felt it was right for us to be together, so they devised a plan. They isolated us from my mother and the Reverend by inviting us on a weekend fishing trip to Wyoming.

We had a wonderful time! It was the most liberated I had felt all summer as we hiked, caught fish, and baked potatoes under the ground. Denny didn't shave, which made my cheeks rosy from smooching as we kissed with no catechism between us. Our last night at the cabin, we stayed up until dawn while Denny and our friends deprogrammed me. By 5:00 A.M., I knew the beliefs of my church were important to my mother — not to me. I probably would need to leave home to find my own way, but I wanted to leave with Denny.

When our three days ended, Denny returned to Nebraska and I brave-ly returned home. I was ready to tell my mother I would chance going to hell, no matter what God thought, because he was unfair. I still thought God was a man.

My mother did not take this well and made quite a scene. My father stayed out of it and sat in the small kitchen of our rented home, sipping cof-fee and smoking cigarettes. The confrontation between my mother and me intensified, and we were both in tears by the time I decided to place a long-distance call to Denny. My mother, knowing I would give him my answer, flew into the kitchen, gasping for air, and demanded my father's help. "Butch, Butch! Stop her! [Gasp] She's going to marry him!"

My father was so fed up that he yelled at my mother, "I don't care if she marries a goddamned Catholic!" By that time I was overcome and choking on my tears.

Denny, in Nebraska, was in the middle of a house meeting with twelve, male, pre-theological students whom he supervised in exchange for free rent. When he answered the phone, I could hardly talk. Alarmed, Denny asked, "Betty, what's wrong?" Then he yelled into the mouthpiece, "Will you guys get off the phone?" Whenever we talked long distance, those guys listened, allowing us no privacy whatever. They heard all of our conversations, and this time they heard my mother ranting in the background.

I blubbered, "Denny, do you still want to marry me?" I could hear the eavesdroppers snickering.

"Of course!" he blurted.

"Me too." I was pitiful.

Denny moved fast. "I'll get an engagement ring right away. What size do you wear?"

His question reduced me to whimpers and I weakly answered, "I don't know. I don't care. Whatever fits."

It was done. I had taken my future into my own hands, which meant I might go to hell, but Denny would be with me. I went straight to my bed-room, slammed the door, and cried from relief. My father poured bourbon, and my mother took a Phenobarbital to pull herself together. She was no doubt pale as she dialed the phone to schedule another meeting with the Reverend.

This time the Reverend knew I was determined and didn't care where I got married or who married us. He finally said, "All right, Betty. To avoid your excommunication, I will marry you in this church on *one* condition."

"Yes, what?" I was alert.

He hunched forward as though whispering a secret. "You must do everything in your power to convert Denny *after* your marriage."

"Absolutely! That was my plan!" That big fat lie was so believable that I could have received an award for it.

There were a few more kinks to smooth before a ceremony with an "outsider" could be performed, but they were minor compared to the hurdle we had cleared that summer. Of course, I never kept my promise to the Reverend, because I had my fingers crossed the whole time.

Denny took me as a bride to that house with the twelve pre-theological students, where they listened to our conversations through the walls and left notes that read, "Your bedroom is wired."

Residing in a small college town where Denny was the youngest person on the faculty, we joined a local house of worship where the members didn't even know about the reserved seats in heaven, and I thanked God for that.

My mother's breath returned and she forgave Denny for taking me away, but she never told the Reverend that I joined a different church. God didn't seem to mind. In fact, for the next forty-nine years, She blessed our union.

Thanksgiving Wedding

When our family gathered for our traditional Thanksgiving dinner in 1997, we knew it might be the last one with Denny. He knew it, too, and ended his dinner blessing by saying: "Lord, if this is as close as we get to heaven on earth, then I'm satisfied. Amen."

When I affectionately stroked his hairless arm, I noticed the slight jaundiced color of his skin, which seemed to have happened overnight. I watched as Denny carved the turkey, which had been prepared by a neighborhood restaurant to minimize his aversion to cooking odors. The effects of his cancer treatments were becoming too obvious to ignore.

I couldn't help thinking back to our first Thanksgiving together, two days before we were married in 1949. Some of Denny's family had arrived from Kansas, just in time for dinner. My family was financially strapped and didn't have the means to purchase a turkey that would feed a crowd in addition to paying for a $150 wedding. But, my mother had a creative way with food and molded a huge meat loaf into the shape of a roasted turkey. It was a wonderful meal with all the usual Thanksgiving trimmings, minus the bird. My future family appreciated the good food and the humor with which it was offered.

In spite of having little money, we had a lovely wedding. Mom and I made my taffeta gown, complete with a train, zillions of loops, and hand-covered buttons that ran up the long sleeves and down the front of the bodice. It took forever to make all those loops and buttons, but even longer to button them.

My veil was a gift from a neighbor who created accessories for a bridal shop. We still had some other expenses to cover when Denny and I actually found a $20 bill on the sidewalk in downtown Englewood. We assumed it was a gift from God to pay for our flowers.

In addition to these many blessings, it seemed we might even save on Denny's haircut by following my father's advice. He announced, "My barber offered to cut the groom's hair for free. Just tell him I sent ya." What a deal! We couldn't pass up that one. Denny went straight to the barbershop and announced he was the guy who was marrying Butch Peal's daughter. The barber's only response was, "Congratulations! How nice. Where ya from?" It was awkward, to be sure, so Denny paid $2 for the worst haircut of his life. It was shaved high up on the back of his head and straight across the bottom like an old-fashioned bowl cut — not at all stylish in 1949. From the back it looked terrible, and that's primarily what the congregation would see. I was anxious for people to notice that his face was better than his hair.

We had other wrinkles that needed smoothing. Denny's father was a minister and had performed the weddings for all of his other children. But, because of restrictions in my church, he would not be allowed to assist in our ceremony. Undaunted, Denny was determined to find a way his dad could play an important role in our wedding. He demoted his best man to head usher. Then, my sixteen-year old brother was demoted from head usher to just plain usher, and Reverend Auchard became his son's best man.

However, the wedding events were not without more anxieties. Our rented house had a major sewer problem the week before our wedding. My dad was determined to fix it himself and dug a deep pit exposing our ailing septic tank, which was now bordered by a mountain of stinky dirt. I assumed this would be corrected before my wedding day. It wasn't, and the whole neighborhood smelled like excrement, which is a nice word for poop.

Our toilets wouldn't flush, and we couldn't use the bathtub. So, on the day of my wedding my family of five took turns bathing in a tin tub in the warm kitchen. Mom heated a boiler on the stove and kept adding fresh, hot water to the tub for each new bather. Since I was the bride, I was allowed to choose my bathing order. I could have gone first with just three inches in which to wash, but I chose to immerse in deeper, slightly used water so I went last. It allowed me to shave my legs high up above my knees, where I had never shaved before, so I would be wonderfully smooth everywhere on my wedding night. It gave me a rash.

Finally, my hair and makeup were complete. Perfume, deodorant, and wedding garter were in place, as well as something old, new, borrowed, and blue. My ultra sheer nylon hose were eased onto my legs with glove-covered hands. Then came the taffeta gown with all those loops and hand-covered buttons. It was truly a robing ritual. My legs and skin felt oddly smooth all over, even where I had not shaved. Oh, Lord! It was then I realized my slip was still on the bed instead of on me. We had no time to unhook and rehook a zillion covered buttons, so my mother got a seam ripper and picked out the two side seams of my gown. She then pulled the slip up from below, cut off the straps, stitched the slip to the top of my bra, and hand-sewed the side seams back together from the outside.

We were now actually late for my wedding, and I was beginning to feel sweaty with anxiety. We were breathless when my family of five finally got to the church. The music had repeated several times, and I had broken my deodorant barrier. The guests were visibly relieved as we arrived, and they settled into their pews as the ceremony proceeded. I heard the Reverend's voice, but wasn't really listening. I was vaguely preoccupied with thoughts of my hastily attached slip. Would it hold? I also wondered how Denny's hair looked from behind.

I repeated my vows quietly and watched Denny's lips move as he repeated his. I wouldn't be able to kiss those lips until we were alone. Kissing during a wedding ceremony was not part of my church's practice, but whatever we said and did allowed us to become man and wife. We had our pictures taken by everyone, and I found frequent opportunities to explain Denny's bad haircut, as if people gave a hoot, which they didn't. Our wedding guests were mostly impressed with my twenty-three-year-old guy from Kansas for his unpretentious manner and stunning good looks. He was remarkably handsome and likable. I was so proud to be marrying him.

Our reception was held in my parent's rented house outside of historic Fort Logan. The event was nothing upscale, just cake, punch, and coffee in a warm, crowded, happy atmosphere. But I was praying so hard, "God, please don't let anyone use the toilet since it won't flush, and puhleeeze don't let the whole neighborhood smell like poop!" And that night, for some miraculous reason, no one used the toilet and the neighborhood did not smell like poop. God is good.

We opened our gifts and mingled with guests, enjoying refreshments while my dad sat in the kitchen being a good host to my new father-in-law. Being a good host meant offering Reverend Auchard a shot of whiskey so the dads could drink a toast to the newlyweds. Denny's father declined the liquor, but graciously raised a cup of punch alongside my dad's bourbon glass. No doubt he was also offering a silent prayer for all of us.

Meanwhile, my brother stuffed potatoes in the exhaust pipe of Denny's coupe and tied a million tin cans to the bumper. He must have saved tin cans for a month. My teen-aged brother and sister had a ball during the celebration, my father had his occasional shot of whiskey, Denny's folks had the Lord on their side, and Denny and I had each other.

We stayed that night in the Brown Palace Hotel in Denver, returning the next day to have more pictures taken and give my brother a serious lecture regarding potatoes in the exhaust pipe. Then we collected our wedding gifts and all my earthly possessions, which included my violin, love letters, yearbooks, photos, dolls, artwork, and two foot-long braids that had been cut from my head only three years earlier.

For reasons I didn't understand, the simple act of packing up all of my personal belongings was a real shock to my mother. I was barely nineteen and the first child to leave home, so it must have been hard for her to see me leave. My mother struggled with the realization that I was uprooting myself for good.

I hugged and kissed everybody, and Denny assured my parents he would take care of me always. I promised to write as we drove away, but I could still see my mother and sister crying, my brother waving his hands off, and my father smiling as I left my family forever.

My family was sad to see me leave, but I was ecstatic as I headed east with my brand new husband to start married life in York, Nebraska. And what a good life it was for almost forty-nine years.

※ ※ ※

"Betty, do you want light meat or dark?" I had been away and Denny's question brought me back to the present.

"Oh, whatever's on top, Hon," I said as I sipped my white wine and passed the cranberries around.

Denny barely touched his plate. The food looked appealing but his appetite was poor. In spite of that, he was very happy that last Thanksgiving with us. He lightheartedly commented to our daughter, "Renee, if I'm still around next year, I plan to eat everything in sight!"

Denny's Special Powers
In our family, Denny was the conjurer who found lost things. When he realized that one of us was on a hunt for missing glasses or a wallet, he would set aside whatever he was doing and slyly join the search. After secretly locating the missing article, Denny might announce with no fanfare, "I'm getting vibrations from a wallet. Are you guys looking for one?"

"OK, Dad. Where is it?" Dave would ask.

"I don't know yet," Denny would reply. Then he would close his eyes and touch his fingertips to his temples, saying, "Wait a minute. I'm getting a message." After a few moments of intense concentration, he would reveal the location of the lost object. "Look . . . on the night stand . . . in the guest bedroom." Then his knees would buckle as he grasped a wall for support, staggered to the nearest chair, and gasped, "I've gotta rest." Sometimes he pretended to be temporarily blinded by the effort, whimpering, "Where is everybody?"

Despite the drama, Denny was, indeed, the master of finding lost things — far better than the rest of us. In fact, we counted on him, and we usually didn't commit ourselves fully to the hunt because we knew he would cover our carelessness with his "special powers." But the best part was watching that funny little routine because Denny wasn't a silly kind of guy. He revealed that part of himself only after he'd had a couple of jiggers of scotch — or when something got lost.

Dirty Towel Tricks
Denny was tidy, organized, selective, quiet, responsible, loving, and cautious — VERY cautious. There wasn't a spontaneous bone in his body. He would never have spoken the words, "Let's make it up as we go along." He took a chance on nothing and tried new things only if they came highly recommended by those he trusted.

Denny made decisions after researching for several weeks, then making a contract in triplicate for all parties to sign. It took a long time — and a lot of patience — whenever we hired someone to build a fence or paint the house.

There was no limit to his caution. It spilled over into mundane areas such as buying groceries or eating out. After returning home, we often compared each item in the grocery bags against our receipt. He never paid a restaurant tab without checking the math. I fully expected him to write a grade in red ink on the automatically printed receipt along with, "Well done, machine."

Sometimes he actually found glaring errors in handwritten bills, and that sort of success spurred him on. He did not like people, let alone machines, taking advantage of him or being careless with our money. Whenever I saw him in a long discussion with a cashier, I wandered near the phone booth and pretended to read the instructions for inserting coins. If the conversation between Denny and a clerk grew testy, I disappeared into the ladies' room.

It was terribly embarrassing, but Denny believed in protecting himself. For a quiet, gentle man, he had a slightly macho side — not in a tough way, but a stubborn way. As irritating as it was, I got used to his habits and had my own way of making fun of them behind his back. For example, I played dirty towel tricks.

Denny was fussy about bath towels. He used two each day — one for the top half of his body and the other for the bottom half. His towels took up a lot of space on our racks. I didn't need much space for my one towel.

He often said to me, "Betty, I don't see how you can use the same towel on your whole body."

Each time I replied, "My whole body is clean after I've taken a bath."

He once responded, "I know, but sometimes I think that's what causes our colds."

"Oh, Denny, I don't think that's what causes our colds at all."

"Well, you don't know that for sure," he replied. "And it doesn't hurt to be careful."

Denny was careful about not dropping his towels on the closed toilet seat or, God forbid, the floor. If one slipped onto either of those surfaces, he wouldn't use it until it was laundered again. I protested, "Honey, I just scrubbed the toilet and floor this morning. They're clean."

His answer was always the same: "Well, you don't know that for sure, and it doesn't hurt to be careful."

His fear of germs annoyed me, but there was no way to reason with him. I made fun of it privately, though he never knew it. Whenever he was out of town on business, I had my way with his towels.

While Denny was gone, I went beyond the limits to flout the towel rules. After a shower, I purposely dried every part of my body with two towels — his — and then I dropped them on the toilet seat and floor before hanging them on his racks to dry.

When Denny returned home, unpacked his bags, and took a shower, he usually asked, "Betty, are these towels clean?"

I pretended to think very hard and then lied casually, "Yeah, they sure are." I got impish pleasure from watching him innocently dry his wet body with towels that had dried every crevice of my own body and then landed on the toilet seat and floor several times. I was *so* bad.

I think about Denny a lot these days, and our collection of towels gets used very little. I'm *never* out of towels, and they will last the rest of my life. If Denny were still alive, I would give him all the clean towels he wanted, and I would never play dirty towel tricks on him again.

But I could be wrong.

Printing Wild Grass

While visiting relatives in Kansas who grew wheat and raised cattle, Denny and I were shown a huge patch of marijuana growing wild in their draw. The foliage towered ten feet, branching high over our heads. I asked to have my photo taken standing next to the plants to prove their height. I then pinched a small leaf and placed it gently on the floor of the car for the drive back to their farm. I couldn't believe my good luck to have found *Cannabis sativa* and looked forward to printing it in Nature Printing Journal #3. I announced with pride, "I picked a marijuana leaf to print in my botanical journals."

The reaction was immediate, resembling controlled panic. My sister-in-law said, "Toss it!"

"Toss it? Why?"

"It's against the law to transport marijuana in the state of Kansas."

"But this is for educational purposes, a scientific experience."

"It's not worth the risk. THROW IT OUT. QUICK!"

Reluctantly, I obliged, but I grumbled under my breath. The disappointment was hard to shake even while eating fresh corn on the cob and steaks to die for.

A few days later my husband and I camped in western Iowa where I took my usual stroll through untamed brush in search of unusual plants to print. I swatted mosquitoes and stepped in deer poop but, to my surprise, I encountered wild marijuana growing in abundance in the thickets near our site. With much excitement, I pinched a leaf and brazenly transported it to our motor home. I used the pages of an old telephone book to protect the illegal specimen. I knew that Denny would be edgy with it in our rig, so I didn't share my plan with him. I would make secret prints with my marijuana leaf as soon as he fell asleep that night.

Both sides of the cannabis sample made beautiful images, and I worked through the night. I printed it repeatedly in letters to our four children, then on fabric, and finally in the pages of *Journal #3*. After so much pressing, the sacrificial leaf was sadly bruised and had released its concentrated, intoxicating fragrance into our cramped quarters. It surprised me that the strong odor of "pot" didn't awaken Denny.

I cleaned up my tiny "art studio" space on top of the stove and packed away my watercolors and journals. Then I cracked the windows to freshen the air. I was so happy to have finally made prints of the notorious marijuana leaf that I went to bed with a grateful heart and a Mona Lisa smile on my face.

Perhaps I was high.

First Love: A Conversation with My Dad

My dad and Denny were important men in my life, and they had several things in common. Each had married his first love — and of course, both of them loved me. Even though time and fading health eventually removed most of us from his memory, Dad never forgot his first love: my mother.

My parents loved each other but did not know how to stay together. They married and divorced each other three times. Even after my father's second wife, Lucille, died, my parents stayed friends, and my mother visited him in the convalescent home whenever she went back to Iowa. Dad wanted her to move in with him. My mom said that when she visited him, he couldn't keep his hands off her — and they were both almost 80!

Now, it was my turn to visit my dad in the convalescent home. Denny clutched my sweaty hand as we entered the front door. I hadn't seen my dad in several years and didn't know what to expect. Denny and I waited as they wheeled Dad into the room. I had never seen him in a wheelchair before. He wore a baseball cap with an opening in the back where his faded red hair poked through. His face lit up when he saw us, though not with recognition. I could tell he hadn't the faintest idea who we were. Denny and I introduced ourselves, and Dad plunged headlong into conversation. He still loved to talk to anyone who would listen.

DAD: Now, who did you say you are?

BETTY: I'm Betty, your oldest child, Dad.

DAD: Oh. I couldn't remember if you said you were my sister or my daughter.

BETTY:	Your sister was here today, so maybe that confused you.
DAD:	What's her name?
BETTY:	Her name is Lora, Dad, your oldest sister.
DAD:	Oh. Lora?
BETTY:	Yes, Lora.
DAD:	Yeah, I remember her. She comes to see me sometimes, but I can never remember her name. Where does she live?
BETTY:	She lives in Cedar Rapids, where you used to live.
DAD:	Where do you live?
BETTY:	In California.
DAD:	In California? That's where Waneta is from. Do you know Waneta?
BETTY:	Oh, yes, Dad. I know her well. Waneta is my mother.
DAD:	Well, I'll never forget Waneta. She came to visit me a couple of times.
BETTY:	Oh, yes, she told me about visiting you here.
DAD:	Don't know why in the ever-lovin' world she moved to California. Do you see Waneta much?
BETTY:	Oh, sure. All the time.
DAD:	I'll never forget Waneta.
BETTY:	Well, Dad, you and Mom were married a long time.
DAD:	Well, then, who in the hell is Lucille? Lemme show you this newspaper clipping someone gave me because "Lucille" just died. They say I was married to her!
BETTY:	Yeah, Dad, you were.
DAD:	What was Lucille like?
BETTY:	She was a very nice woman.
DAD:	Well, you couldn't prove it by me.
BETTY:	Dad, you were actually married to Lucille longer than you were married to Mom.
DAD:	And you come from California?
BETTY:	Yes, and you came to visit us a couple of times in California.
DAD:	I seem to remember sitting out under a tree and reading my detective magazines and drinking a beer. Could that have been in California?
BETTY:	It sure was, Dad. You really liked sitting under our mulberry tree.
DAD:	Were the mulberries a mess on the ground?

BETTY: No, we have fruitless mulberries in California.

DAD: Those damned mulberry trees are a mess when the fruit is all over the ground.

BETTY: I remember the huge one we had on Oakland Road in Cedar Rapids.

DAD: The one I remember was such a mess!

BETTY: Bobby fell down under that tree and bit his tongue so bad he had to have five stitches.

DAD: Bobby? I keep remembering the names Betty, Bobby, and Patty.

BETTY: That's us — the three children you and Mom had. I'm Betty, and Bob and Pat are my brother and sister. Pat has red hair, just like you.

DAD: Now, where do they live?

BETTY: Bob lives in Nebraska and Pat lives in Colorado.

DAD: And you live in California?

BETTY: Right. But we all lived in Cedar Rapids 'til I was fourteen. Then you got transferred to the Denver Iron Works and we moved to Colorado. [I was afraid this might be too much input for my dad to process, but I plunged on.] After I got married, Denny and I moved to California in 1956, and we have four children.

DAD: Well, I don't remember them, and I don't remember Lucille, and sometimes I can't even remember which one is my sister.

BETTY: That happens, Dad, when you don't see those people every day.

DAD: I'll tell you one thing for sure!

BETTY: What's that?

DAD: I don't see Waneta every day, but I will never forget her!

BETTY: Well, you were only seventeen when you met and twenty-one when I was born. I don't think you ever forget your first love.

DAD: How long did you say we were married?

BETTY: Close to twenty-seven years.

DAD: I know another thing about Waneta. I know for sure she was a virgin.

BETTY: Oh, really? [Gulp] And how did you know that, Dad?

DAD:	Well, she was living away from home because she didn't get on very well with her mother.
BETTY:	Oh, yes. I know that was true.
DAD:	And Waneta and I met at a young people's group at the Southern Baptist church. We both played cornet in the orchestra.
BETTY:	Your church had an orchestra?
DAD:	No, not the whole church, just the young people's group.
BETTY:	You were both very musically inclined.
DAD:	Inclined, hell. Waneta could make a piano talk!
BETTY:	How right you are, Dad.
DAD:	Anyway, I took a shine to her right off and used to walk her home to where she got free room and board for taking care of the kids in the family after school. Then I would walk all the way to my house, and that was a hell of a lot of walkin' in the snow.
BETTY:	In the snow?
DAD:	Yeah. It was snowin' that night!
BETTY:	Which night, Dad?
DAD:	The night I'm talkin' about. Now, stay with me!
BETTY:	Oh, OK.
DAD:	Anyway, I had been after her to do it for a long time, and she wouldn't.
BETTY:	Do it? You mean . . . like making love?
DAD:	Yeah! Doin' it! The back porch was closed in for the winter with storm windows and wasn't so cold as the outside. [My dad pauses.]
BETTY:	Yes, and . . .
DAD:	Since no one was home, Waneta decided to do it with me.
BETTY:	[Gulp, Gulp] Um hmm.
DAD:	The washer and tubs was the only things out there. Waneta took off her panties, and I lifted her up on the lid of one of them tubs. It had a big knob in the middle that was pressing on her butt, so it took a little doin' to get comfortable, and then we did it on top of the lid of that tub. [My dad seemed lost in thought at this point and didn't talk for several seconds, until I cautiously broke his reverie.]
BETTY:	So, how did you know Mom was a virgin, Dad?
DAD:	[Impatiently] I'm gettin' to it!

BETTY:	OK. [I had been scolded.]
DAD:	Well, I had a few miles to walk all the way home with snow over my ankles and by the time I got there, my ass was freezin'.
BETTY:	Dad, I believe you.
DAD:	I got undressed for bed and went to put my shorts in the hamper and saw blood inside my shorts.
BETTY:	And that's how you could tell that Mom was a virgin?
DAD:	Yup! But I knew I would catch holy hell if my mother saw those shorts with blood in 'em.
BETTY:	What did you do?
DAD:	Well, I found me an old rag, a rock, a paper bag, and some string. Then I wrapped those bloody shorts around that rock, tied it all up real good, put it in the paper bag, tied the paper bag up real good with lots of tight string, and put it in my jacket pocket.
BETTY:	Then what?
DAD:	On my way to the Quaker Oats plant where I worked after I dropped out of school, I had to pass by the slough, and I was thinkin' about throwin' it way out in the middle of the water where it could sink to the bottom.
BETTY:	Oh, do I remember the slough. We swam there on sizzling hot days with all the other poor kids in town.
DAD:	Well, no one, rich or poor, could swim in it this day. It was frozen solid. I wasn't expectin' no ice-covered slough! [I was on the edge of my seat.]
BETTY:	So, what did you do, Dad?
DAD:	Well, I looked both ways real casual, like I was just lookin' over the scenery, and when I saw the coast was clear, I took the package out of my pocket and slung it as hard as I could to get it way out in the middle of the slough where the ice might be thin.
BETTY:	Did it sink?
DAD:	Not right at first, and that really worried me. I didn't want no one gettin' curious and somehow findin' out they was my shorts.
BETTY:	Dad, how would they have ever known that?

DAD: We had ten kids in our family and our names were marked with a laundry marker in all our underwear so we'd know whose shorts was whose!

BETTY: Dad, what about the rock package? Did it ever sink?

DAD: Yeah, it did, but not right at first. It hesitated just a little before it cracked through the ice and disappeared. Boy, was I relieved.

BETTY: Well, I know I'm relieved. Then did you go on to work?

DAD: Yup. I went on to work, but I couldn't get my mind off how Waneta had finally let me do it with her. [Pause] I had never done it before either! I'll never forget it.

BETTY: Oh, I will never forget it either! That was a very dear story, and I'm so glad you told it to me.

DAD: [Nothing but silence, relishing his memory.]

BETTY: They're waiting dinner for you in the dining room, so I'd better get going. We have to drive back to Nebraska tonight, but it was just wonderful being here with you. [I forgot to call him Dad.]

DAD: It's been nice talkin' to you, too. Now, who did you say you are?

BETTY: I'm Betty, your oldest child, Dad, from California.

DAD: [Snaps his fingers] That's right! I keep forgettin'.

Part 3: *Staying Afloat*

Cookie Power

*L*earning to live alone has made me aware of a few things about myself. For instance, I have discovered that I'm compulsive, slob-like, and disorganized — and that cookies are essential to my survival.

Denny and I both loved cookies, and they were a staple in our cupboard. But when he felt we were eating too many, he would wave his hand and say, "Get these cookies out of my sight!" Now that I'm alone, I find every way imaginable to fit them into the healthy food groups without guilt. Cookies are my starch, vegetable, fruit, protein, dairy, and fat.

Sometimes I leap out of bed with such enthusiasm that I don't even bother to dress or eat before starting my tasks. I don't plan it this way (that's disorganized); I'm driven to it (that's compulsive). I don't think twice before I'm on my hands and knees cleaning around the base of the toilets or in the garden grooming the roses. Efficiently, I go from one task to another, still in my nightie, housecoat, and slippers. I get sweatier by the minute (so slob-like) and wonder why I can't get this inspired after I've dressed (really disorganized).

Sometime around noon I pray that no one drops by and finds me in my nightclothes, with a shovel in one hand and a cookie in the other. If the doorbell rings, I plan to answer it and pretend I'm not well. Hopefully, they won't notice that I'm well enough to have cookies on my breath.

The first thing that usually slows me down is legitimate hunger, but it doesn't stop my work in progress. It's only a challenge to see how much I can accomplish before doing the logical things: showering, dressing, eating, and behaving normally. Hunger brings a bit of urgency to my tasks. It's when a headache blooms that I know the only thing standing between me and starvation is, obviously, a cookie. I can get another half-hour of work done with one cookie under my belt. Two cookies and a glass of cold milk, and I'm good for two hours.

I can live on cookies. In fact, if there is a good supply of cookies around, I won't bother to cook real food. I have recently taken to hiding them from myself but, apparently, my memory isn't as bad as I thought.

Some might think, "This woman needs counseling." Not so. I accept that I am a disorganized, compulsive slob — but for that I don't need counseling. What I do need is another cookie or two and a glass of really cold milk. Then I'll get dressed.

Not Ready to Date

Denny and I had purchased the burial location for our cremains several years before he was diagnosed with cancer, but we hadn't gotten around to buying the plan to have us cremated. When Denny grew more ill, he suggested that we contact Norman Dowd, the burial salesman. Norman offered to come to our house to complete the paperwork so a family member could sit with me. Denny was too ill to take part and rested in the family room while Renee, our younger daughter, took his place.

It took almost two hours of paper shuffling and pen pushing. When we were finished, Norman went into the other room to chat with Denny. Then he left. I didn't expect to see Norman again. But one morning, three months after Denny's death, Norman rang my doorbell.

"Hi, Mrs. Auchard," he said in a cheery voice. "I was on my way to work and just thought I'd stop to say hello and see how you're doing."

"Well, hello, Norman. What a surprise," I replied. I was not only surprised, but embarrassed. I'd gotten into the habit of sleeping late and then doing small tasks in my nightgown, housecoat, and slippers before working on my computer until dawn.

The logical solution would have been to ask Norman to come back another time, but I didn't want to hurt his feelings. So I asked him in for coffee, which I hadn't yet fixed for myself. He admired the fact that I ground my own coffee beans, and I didn't like being admired by someone I barely knew while in my sleeping clothes. As we sat at the kitchen table waiting for the coffee to perk, we talked about religion, our children, and the fact that we had both lost a spouse. He told me that he'd been alone for many years.

I shifted uncomfortably in my chair, feeling slightly underdressed for this new subject.

Then he commented that he didn't get along well with his only child, a daughter, and rarely saw her even though she was his only living relative. He sounded pitiful when he said, "I could die in my apartment and no one would miss me for days."After an hour and a half, Norman *finally* rose to leave. As we continued our chat on the front porch, he asked me to go to dinner sometime.

I wasn't surprised. He'd waited for a respectable amount of time to pass before paying me a visit to ask me out. I wasn't ready for that kind of attention, and I didn't know how to handle the invitation. It had been fifty years since a man had asked me for a date and that was when I met Denny. I managed to say, "Oh, I'm not ready for dating, Norman."

"This isn't a date," he said. "You've gotta eat dinner and you may as well eat it with me." I didn't want to hurt his feelings, so I invited him for Thanksgiving dinner when my family would be present. He was thrilled, and I felt worse than ever. I didn't want a gentleman friend any more than I wanted a goldfish or a turtle.

As soon as Norman left, I started weaving a tangled web to get out of being paired with him at Thanksgiving. I approached my friend Marguerite, who really enjoyed dating. I suggested that she join our family at Thanksgiving so she could meet Norman, but she was more cautious than I had been.

"I would love to come to your house for Thanksgiving dinner, but I want to meet him first to see if I like him," she said. I felt hopeful, so I persuaded Norman to visit the store she managed to see if they clicked. They met and chatted between customers. Norman felt a click, but Marguerite did not. She declined my invitation to Thanksgiving dinner, saying, "Sorry, but he's not my type." So I was again going to be paired with Norman at a family gathering — and all because I felt sorry for him.

I was so anxious that I got a cold sore. I shared my feelings with my kids, but they couldn't understand what the big deal was. I didn't know how to explain it to them. I just wasn't ready for a man to be interested in me, not even Robert Redford.

About a week before the holiday meal, it dawned on me that Thanksgiving would have been Denny's and my fiftieth anniversary. With that revelation, I saw my way out of the sticky mess I'd created. First, I made reservations for only my family at a nice local restaurant. Then I called Norman to chicken out of my invitation.

"Please forgive me [and I meant it], but I forgot that this would have been a very special Thanksgiving for Denny and me, so I want to celebrate it with only my family." He was very gracious. My cold sore healed almost overnight.

But Norman didn't give up easily. It took almost six more months of turning him down for dinner dates before I got up the nerve to say, "I'd rather you not call me anymore because I'm just not ready to date."

And I doubted that I ever would be.

The Special Gift

I finally got the Christmas tree decorated today even though my son and his wife put the lights on seven days ago. It hardly mattered that nothing but lights covered my yuletide greenery; the neighbors couldn't tell from the outside that the thing was bare of baubles.

Today, I spent the whole day — it seemed — dressing it, while the Nutcracker Suite repeated seven times on the stereo. Naturally, I danced as it played, breaking a couple of glass ornaments in the process. After a lot of rearranging and starting over more than once, I think the tree looks pretty good and it smells even better. The process of decorating all by myself got me in the spirit of rejoicing that I am here.

It's the very first time in my life that I have decorated a whole Christmas tree without help. Well — I don't count the lights. The lights are the hardest part because it's not easy for an undersized woman like me to arrange a long string of little bulbs up to the top, around the middle, down and behind a tall, fat Douglas fir. A new widow, as short as I, can't control everything in her life.

Later today, our family of sixteen plus two granddaughters' boyfriends, one grandson's girlfriend, and a few pets will gather for our annual Christmas party. This year, only the three little kids have drawn names for the gift exchange. The rest of us will find some possession we no longer want, will wrap it beautifully, and get rid of it in a "grab bag" game of chance. The rules are that each person *must take the "gift" they receive home with them. Then, the cast-off is theirs to do with as they wish.*

※ ※ ※

Now the party has ended, the dishes are done, and all the children, grandchildren, boyfriends, girlfriends, pets, and useless gifts are on their way home. The party was chaotic, noisy, and fun. Three dogs kept us wary, and two three-year-olds kept us watchful. We had enough food for three family gatherings. The highlight of my evening was when one of the teenage dissenters was unusually gracious and hugged his mother and me tightly.

The grab bag allowed us to rid ourselves of bath salts, old videos, free soap, shower caps, hand lotion from motels, and bad purchases made in a hurry. My children laughed about the "gifts" they received. They appreciated that I changed the Christmas gift rules because it prevented stress and cash flow problems for everyone in the family. People tried hard to leave these "gifts" behind but, of course, that was against the rules.

This year, however, there was one present saved for the end and cherished by all. My oldest daughter assembled all 37 of my stories, poems, and essays into a binder for each family so they would have a copy of everything I had written since their dad died eighteen months ago. This special gift no one left behind.

Camping Alone

I knew this place well. The roads leading from one section to another were imprinted on my brain, as this was once our haunt — Denny's and mine. Only a few years ago we owned a motor home and frequently camped on these grounds, if you consider a motor home camping, which we did. Sometimes, our children and their families joined us. We had wonderful times here.

I often dreamed of camping alone for a few days, with only our small black dog, Bridget, to keep me company. It sounded like fun, being away from home and playing house, so I occasionally mentioned it to Denny.

"Why?" he asked. I wasn't sure, but it might have been because I married young. I had never been a single girl and wanted to see what it was like. But Denny failed to understand why I thought camping alone would be fun, so I never got around to doing it until now — now that he's gone.

Yesterday, I settled into a rented trailer with food, sleeping bag, and laptop computer. I gave Bridget away when Denny became ill, but I had Tina, my small white terrier, to keep me company. I really looked forward to this experience. But once I arrived, it seemed more strange than fun, alone with a bitchy little dog that Denny never knew.

Tina has a very dominant personality. If she had been born human, she might have held a high position in a corporate office in one of those tall buildings in San Francisco. Tina wants it all and is rarely intimidated. I felt safe with her at my side.

Last night after dark, when the campground seemed settled, I took Tina for a walk. It was a doggie smorgasbord! She was beside herself with anticipation at every bush and tree trunk. Lifting her leg like a male, she almost fell over backward trying to mark higher than any dog before her. She marked territory so frequently that I wondered when her pee reservoir would run dry.

Tina and I covered most of the park. The darkness exuded moist, earthy odors that I could taste. A few open curtains revealed couples playing cards or watching television, if they had a satellite dish on their rig. Darkened campsites offered testimony that most campers were cozily tucked in for the night. Occasionally, a tethered dog barked, protecting its territory as we strolled, bringing Tina's neck hairs to attention.

I passed many spots where Denny and I had hooked up our rig and set up our awning, and the memories came too easily. Tears welled every time I recognized one of our old campsites. I wasn't prepared for the lonely feeling that wrapped itself around me. I was alone and Denny was gone, but his presence was so real that I imagined his hand in mine. I could almost feel it.

We rounded a corner onto a new lane, and I was jerked back to reality when I heard barking dogs running fast at us from the dark. Then I saw them — two huge malamutes coming straight for Tina.

Tina was flipping all over the place at the end of the leash, pulling me with her. Barks shrieked from her throat. The sounds of three fighting dogs split the night. The ruckus brought sleepy campers out of their tents and trailers. I was terrified.

My dog was fast and fierce, and her hairs were standing up so straight that I hardly recognized her. Those bully dogs didn't know they were messing with a bitch that had tried to pee higher than any stud before her. I yelled "No!" in my deepest voice while Tina thrashed between them, holding her own.

She was prepared to break their ankles if she had to. It seemed like hours before the dogs' owner rushed out, called them off, and apologized all over the place. She was anxious when she asked, "Is your dog all right?"

"She's fine. She's fine," I insisted. "I'll just keep moving!" I tried hard not to sound scared, but I was terrified!

We walked fast to get away, with Tina huffing leftover snarls and her neck hairs not yet flat. I stopped under one of the dim street lamps to make sure she wasn't injured. Her back was covered with saliva where the giant dogs had their mouths on her, but she was unhurt. It took several minutes before my heart stopped pounding, as we made our way to the safety of our trailer.

Tina was still grumbling when my thoughts returned to how much I had wanted to come here by myself and Denny's reluctance to encourage me. He knew I could get into this kind of trouble and hoped to protect me. I am finally camping on my own and missing him like crazy, with nothing but a bitchy fifteen-pound dog for protection. I guess camping alone isn't all it's cracked up to be.

Men in My House

People ask me all the time, "How are you doing?" Well, when you start life over alone at sixty-eight, it depends on the day. Right when I begin to feel self-confident and cocky, thinking that I'm getting the hang of things, there's an experience just waiting to happen to me. I must admit that it makes me very leery of kicking back too long. I remain alert, uncertain, and edgy, wondering what I've forgotten. Months of home improvement projects have exposed my inability to act like I know what I'm doing. When issues come up that I don't understand, I say to the man I've hired, "I'll have to think about it."

"Thinking about it" means calling my sons for advice and then pretending it's my own idea. Topics such as fence construction, insulation, attic fans, and contracts take time, money, and a willingness to learn. Denny would have taken care of those issues, but they're my responsibility now. I'm the one who must keep my home sound if I want to stay in it, which I do. I'm comfortable here, but I'm uncomfortable with this aspect of widowhood.

When working with tradesmen, glitches happen that test me, and it takes three days to get something irksome off my mind. Every time I sign a contract with new craftsmen, I pray that they know what they're doing and that I find no fault with the job. But I don't trust that possibility, so I've learned to hover without offending as they saw, staple, and hammer their way through my home. I'm always courteous and attentive to their needs, providing them with a toilet and cold drinks. While they're in the john or getting something out of their trucks, I check their work. It's my duty, but I never know what to look for.

The most recent project in this house ends very soon; new carpet will be installed on the stairs, in the hall, and in my bedroom. I tore all the rest out, revealing virgin oak floors. I love it, but Denny would have hated it. To him, bare floors were equivalent to poverty, and you got as much mileage out of a rug as possible. You didn't install a new one just to redecorate. But after thirty-six years, I'd gotten my money's worth out of our gold shag carpet.

Once the stairs, hall, and bedroom floors are covered, I won't be sharing my space with hired men anymore. But I can't stop looking at those shabby kitchen cabinets, wondering what they would look like in natural maple.

Plumber's Helper

I'd had one plumbing problem after another and finally had to cave in and hire someone to come to my aid. The man who breezed into my house introduced himself as "Bo, the plumber." At first he seemed gruff and unfriendly, but I was convinced it was a false front. While giving me a lecture on the problems of old houses and garbage disposals, he made every effort to unplug my kitchen sink.

"Don't ever use lye to unplug your system," he grumbled. "It causes more problems than it helps. Instead, use chlorine bleach once a week to keep the drains open and clean, and never ever use your garbage disposal for anything but rinsing off dirty dishes."

"Really? Why not?" I couldn't believe what I was hearing. My garbage disposal was brand new!

"Houses this old got tree roots cloggin' the sewer lines, and you should have 'em drilled out once a year."

I sighed, fearing the worst and not knowing what kind of expenses might be ahead.

Bo did his best to open my kitchen drain with an electric snake, but he finally declared that he would have to come back another day and bring his helper. My Drano treatment had created garbage Jell-O out of the blockage that was causing the backup of musty water not only in my kitchen sink but the downstairs shower, as well. I didn't want to wait another day with this foul-smelling stuff sitting in the drain, so I spoke up.

"Bo, why can't I be your helper?"

"I was hopin' you'd ask," he replied. "So — where's yer bleach?"

I produced a gallon of Clorox from the laundry, and Bo poured half of it down the drain. He let it sit for fifteen minutes while we chatted about sewers and toilets and waited for a pot of water to boil. He then poured boiling water into the drain and we both hovered over the sink, peering into the black hole with a flashlight and hoping for a sign of water movement. It was too slow for Bo, so we repeated the treatment, finishing off the bleach. That time, right after the boiling water was poured into the drain, we saw a slight bubbling. Bo grabbed the plunger and we flew into action.

My job was to crouch under the kitchen sink and squeeze the vise pliers on the rubber hose from the garbage disposal. It gave Bo the pressure he needed to use the plunger on my stopped-up drain. Just before starting, he gave a quick little bleach speech.

"Remember that there's nothing like bleach to keep these drains open. Yer about to witness a miracle."

As I squatted down to pinch the pliers on the plastic tube, I unexpectedly broke wind. I was horrified. "Oh, no," I thought. "I hope it doesn't smell." But it did, and the odor drifted up past my nose.

Bo was plunging the stopped-up drain with all his might. He worked up a heavy sweat as stale water squirted out of the air vent near the faucets. By that time, my flatulence must have reached Bo's nose. He said breathlessly, but with excitement, "Smell that sewer gas? BLEACH WILL TAKE CARE OF THAT!"

It made me laugh to myself, which caused another silent "puff" of wind to escape. Bo assumed it was sewer gas, as well, and let it pass. I was grateful for his wrong assumption, but even more grateful when he reported that a funnel of fast-moving water had finally formed at the drain. It meant the drain was unplugged. Bo's bleach and boiling water formula was a success, and he was right — I had, indeed, witnessed a miracle; maybe two.

Birthday Bonus

My family was arriving later in the evening to celebrate my seventieth birthday. But I didn't feel so hot, so I was in bed with a scratchy throat and headache as I read a short story by John Steinbeck. I felt awfully tired, probably from dealing with all the plumbing problems I'd had lately. The phone rang on my nightstand, and I innocently answered it. A saleswoman from *Reader's Digest* wanted to send me a free book and needed to confirm my address.

I sighed, used a bookmark to keep my place, and put my short story down while she went on and on. She finally ended her pitch with, "... and if you decide you want the rest of the books in the series, we'll send them to you once a month."

"No, thank you," I replied.

"What's wrong?" she asked. (I thought she was referring to my scratchy, hoarse voice.)

"You mean, what's wrong with me?"

"No. What's wrong with this offer?"

"I'm just not interested."

She paused briefly, and then continued. "We've come out with a new group of authors that I'm sure you will enjoy."

The lady was not going to give up easily, but I didn't feel like hanging up. Hanging up on a person upsets me, and I would much rather resolve a conflict graciously, even with a "telemarketeer." I remained patient as she continued.

"Is it that you don't like the *Reader's Digest* condensed books?" That was an easy one to answer.

"That's right. I really don't like them."

She gasped as though I had just refused a million dollars. I wanted her to say that she would remove me from the list. She hesitated, and then asked, "What about Denny?"

"What about Denny?" I replied. She just wouldn't quit.

"Would he be interested in this free book offer?"

Her question caught me off guard. I almost said that Denny wasn't home, but what came out was, "Denny's dead." I was blunt on purpose.

"OH! I didn't know! I'll remove your name from our list."

"Well, thank you." I hung up.

Denny was the one who had ordered all those *Reader's Digest* condensed books when we got married fifty years ago. He never read them. He liked the way they looked on the library shelves.

The same was true of *National Geographic*. After his death, I gave away forty years of *National Geographic*. I schlepped twenty-four copies at a time to local hospitals in doubled plastic grocery bags. It took weeks to get rid of them because they were so heavy. Sick people loved to look at the stunning photography and the bare-naked natives between the shiny, bright yellow covers of that magazine.

But no one would take all of my *Reader's Digest* condensed books at one time. They wanted only a few of them. That was no good, because the remaining books needed to be propped up. They supported each other. They wouldn't look nice on my bookshelves half down and half up, and Denny's "library look" would be spoiled. I'm probably stuck with them until I die.

My thoughts drifted back to the odd conversation with the saleswoman on the phone and it made me smile. She had been flustered with embarrassment when I told her the man of the house was dead, but I didn't feel one bit sorry for her. I loved the shocked sound in her voice. She will not be able to sell Denny one more thing.

That night my family celebrated my birthday downstairs without me. Even though I felt really ill, I finally joined them to see my cake, laden with fiery candles, and have my picture taken. That's a photo I'll always cherish. Along with my nightgown, housecoat, and party hat, I wore an expression as proud as a peacock — all because I had ruffled the feathers of a telemarketing chick.

My Way

If Denny were still alive, he would not have done what I just did — invite our son Dave, his family, and their big black dog to live with me while they search for a home. Several additional bodies, an extra dog, and countless boxes of belongings would have been far too disruptive for Denny. He would have aided their quest for home ownership in a more businesslike way — a way that involved a spreadsheet, personal loan, low interest rate, papers to sign, and lots of agreements.

Denny was cautious and thorough. He always spent more time making up his mind than I did. But I only needed three days to make this decision. I thought about how empty this big house was with only my little dog as a companion and how good the presence of family sounded. As a bonus, I could let my gardener and handyman go. I made the decision with my heart, because I didn't know how to prepare a spreadsheet or a loan. I know it's not a sound way to make a decision, but I have always been more inclined than Denny to take a chance.

Now that they are here, our home has taken on an air of cozy clutter. The sheer volume of their belongings is more than storage could hold, and it now fills the garage and has spilled into the house and side yard. In spite of the mountain of extra "stuff," we're managing to function. I don't mind boxes stacked everywhere, the intimately rearranged living room, and the extra fence in the back yard that keeps their big dog off my new lawn. It's only temporary. The washing machine that runs most of the time can be replaced when it gives out. Things are falling into place, as I knew they would.

The only dark cloud is that I imagine Denny would disapprove. Our priorities weren't usually the same, and it often took much discussion to reach common ground. If he were here right now, I can hear him saying, "Bet-ty! For crying out loud! What are you doing?" I can see him in the middle of this untidy scene, and I know that he would have been a nervous wreck. I would have been stressed knowing that he was.

An incident took place that made me feel that Denny could have supported my decision. I heard the skill saw running in the shop and figured Dave was up to something. Denny used to drop whatever he was doing to fix broken stuff, and Dave had the same habit.

After a while Dave called to his wife, "Nola, come look!" The excitement in his voice reminded me so much of his dad that I lifted my head in anticipation. Whenever Denny completed a project, he called me out to the shop to see it. How I miss that!

I automatically joined Nola to have a look. Dave had constructed a sturdy, safe "riser" for their little camp stove. Nola and I admired the contraption as Dave explained his method for securing the stove to the base. What a familiar scene this was! I couldn't help but say, "It looks like Dad is back!"

Without lifting his head, Dave replied, "He never left."

Dave's easy statement stayed with me. It certainly feels as though Denny is still here. I think of him every time I write a check or hire someone to work at our house. He probably had more faith in me than I thought he did, or I couldn't have gone forward so easily with this commune-like arrangement with our son, his family, their big dog, and all their earthly possessions compressed into one dwelling. I made this important decision on my own.

Over a year ago, as I rested beside Denny on the bed, I attempted to tell him how I felt about the future when I said, "Honey, I'm not afraid to be alone after you're gone. I'll be all right. It's just that I'm going to miss you so much." He wasn't comfortable showing emotion, but we both cried a little that night. If he were here right now, it's possible that he would say, "Betty, I'm so glad you're the one helping Dave's family this way, because I couldn't have handled it!"

He would have been right. But this is my way, and I can.

Conversation with Dave

DAVE:	Mom, where are you?
BETTY:	In here.
DAVE:	At the computer again?
BETTY:	Yeah.
DAVE:	Why are you at the computer all day long?
BETTY:	I read mail.
DAVE:	All day?
BETTY:	Off and on.
DAVE:	Well, you must get a lot of mail!
BETTY:	Looks that way.
DAVE:	You should get out of this house and do something else!
BETTY:	Probably.
DAVE:	Do you ever do anything else?
BETTY:	Oh, sure.

DAVE:	What?
BETTY:	I eat.
DAVE:	What else besides eat?
BETTY:	I sleep.
DAVE:	And that's it?
BETTY:	Just about.
DAVE:	If Dad were alive, he'd be shocked at all this e-mail.
BETTY:	I don't think so.
DAVE:	Why not?
BETTY:	Because Dad sends most of it, four or five times a day.
DAVE:	Dad never wanted e-mail.
BETTY:	He does now, and he gave me permission to do what I want every day.
DAVE:	Yeah, like you need permission.
BETTY:	My point exactly.

Proof of Life after Death

My mother died thirteen years ago and my husband, only three. But a hail of mail still arrives addressed to each of them, which causes me to think of them often. Some of the letters are just ads. Others are reminders from organizations to which they once belonged that read, "To receive our annual report, please pay your dues. We miss you."

Denny would laugh if he knew that the memorial park where he's buried still sends him advertisements for their "layaway plan." He even used to chuckle at "serious" junk mail such as literature from Planned Parenthood urging him to be cautious before making a baby.

"Too late for that," said Den. "They should have sent this warning four kids ago."

And letters still arrive for my mother from Lane Bryant, the clothing supplier for large women. Although she lost weight, she could never get off the "big ladies" mailing list.

"Don't they know that I'm thin now and can shop anywhere that I please?" she railed. It would make her even madder if she knew that she's still on their preferred customer list when she has no need for clothing of any size.

Since neither mother nor husband can respond to mail that used to annoy them, I toss it in the plastic bin called the "dead letter office." From there the paper will be dumped into a truck and sent to a factory to be torn to shreds, soaked in bleach, and made into mash for a recycled paper that will take colored ink and new words of hype in large type. I might see those letters again, now bearing news of a cruise for Mom or tidings of great joy for Denny — but only if he donates to the stray animals at the pound.

I imagine my mother saying to my husband, "Why in the hell do they keep sending this stuff? We're gone for good."

I've notified companies and organizations, saying, "These people are deceased. Please remove them from your mailing list." And they reply, "Oh, I'm sorry. We'll do that." But the junk mail keeps coming, and now I'm getting used to it. Mom and Denny may be gone, but they'll never leave this house for good. The mailman won't allow it.

Bed Writing

I am happiest when reading and writing in bed, especially in the winter. I don't do it often. It's not laziness, but necessary work that I do for my soul. There are no chores, just a day for silence.

The light must be exact, coming over my shoulder from the large window behind my head. I'll make notes in the book's margins or in one of my small spiral tablets. I'll go inward, reflecting on the words and thoughts of others who did what I'm doing. Only then can I hear what I will write.

Moving Day

Two days before Christmas, Dave, Nola, and Brianna began their move to a "manger" of their own. Yesterday morning, I noticed the dismantled beds in their rooms, and the reality of it stabbed my heart. It was like serving notice that they would soon be gone.

There's no frenzy like moving. We'll take one load after another and fill the single-car garage with stacks of boxes that will probably slop over into the house. And in the excitement of helping them, I'll briefly forget my dread of being alone in this big house again.

I'll miss Nola most of all, for we shared woman talk and laughter until we were weak. We also shared the laundry, cooking, and personal foibles that men don't show to each other. I'll miss her reminders that I have something cooking on the stove or a baby-sitting appointment with my youngest granddaughter. I'll especially miss asking my favorite question: "Nola, what day is this?"

When I first asked that absent-minded question, she responded with kind and gentle "make-believe" patience.

"Betty . . . today is Saturday." Still acting like a caregiver, she added, ". . . and the next day is . . . Sunday." It made us laugh, and that frequently asked question became our first inside joke.

Another incident that still makes us giggle was the day the television almost gave me a heart attack. I was standing too close to the kitchen TV when a violent action scene detonated within inches of my head. I leaped spastically, which also caused Nola to jump. We were airborne within milliseconds of each other. We laughed so hard that we fell limp against the kitchen counter gasping for breath, each of us thinking the other looked the weirdest.

"I swear to God, Betty, you must have jumped two feet off the floor."

"YOU, TOO!"

A different time, we got ridiculous when she knocked on my office door to ask me a question. In my haste to say, "Yes what is it come in or whatever," nothing but a distorted assortment of noises spewed forth.

"What was THAT?" she asked.

"I'm not sure," I replied, "but it felt like a short circuit between my brain and my tongue."

That garbled sound became our typical response to a question when we didn't know the answer. I wish I knew how we spelled it so we could pass it down to our grandchildren. It might have been "SZWADISSITKMN," but we agree that's not quite right, so we're still working on it.

Once they're gone, the fence in the back yard, which kept their big dog off my new lawn, will come down. My garage will once again hold my car, and there are lots of other spaces I'll reclaim. I can go back to slopping around in my housecoat 'til noon and eating all the cookies I want. I'll get used to being here by myself and, maybe, even grow to like it better than I did before they came to live here five months ago.

But once in a while I must phone Nola to ask what day it is so she can answer me patiently, in that silly, calm voice that implies she's talking to a slow child: "Tuesday — today is Tuesday." And I'll need to call her to ask a dumb question so she can spew out that weird collection of syllables that makes us both laugh, the noise that we don't know how to spell.

Maybe I'll take a casserole over occasionally — like every week — and they'll ask me to stay for dinner. Yes, I'd like that, too.

Conversation with Myself

Betty: Oh, man! It's late! I've gotta get up and get dressed.

Myself: Wait! Not yet! I'm still thinking.

BETTY:	I know, I know. That's why I'm still in bed.
MYSELF:	But this is important!
BETTY:	It always is! What now?
MYSELF:	We have twenty-six letters in our alphabet, right?
BETTY:	I know that! I've got to get up!
MYSELF:	The point is coming.
BETTY:	I hope so.
MYSELF:	Think of the infinite number of words formed by only twenty-six letters.
BETTY:	That's why we have dictionaries.
MYSELF:	But think of what can still be said by putting words together in new ways.
BETTY:	That's why we have libraries filled to the ceiling with new books.
MYSELF:	And magazines, bulletins, and all those articles, ads, reports, and statistics.
BETTY:	As well as letters, announcements, wills, and poems?
MYSELF:	Yes! Yes! Do you think the human race will ever run out of things to write about?
BETTY:	I don't believe that could ever happen!
MYSELF:	Wanna lie around and think up some more interesting stuff?
BETTY:	Can't. I've got to get up and write this down.
MYSELF:	Write what down?
BETTY:	What you just said!
MYSELF:	Good idea.

Killing an Hour at the Car Wash

I watch, read, and write as I wait for my Toyota. It's in the car beauty shop. Living outdoors for six months has taken its toll. If the car police could see my "ride," they would take possession and I'd find myself in car court. When the judge noticed the tinted windows covered with bird stuff, he'd send me away for car-owner therapy, even though my insurance does not cover counseling. I know that my auto is a mess, but do I care?

Today I *do* care. My garage is finally free of trappings that don't belong to me, so my car can crash in its own bedroom. And finding a discount coupon for a car makeover encouraged me to be an accountable and caring owner. I removed water bottles, empty soda cans, used tissues, books, magazines, and maps so the car-cleaning guys can get right to work, whistling while they do so.

The front-gate fellow beckons me to pull forward and asks which service I want.

I reply, "I want the big deal job."

"The big *detail* job?" he asks.

"I don't know what it's called, but I want everything done to this car that you can do at this place. I want the works, and I want to know how much this discount coupon will do for me."

"Not much," he answers. "On the full detail job, you get five dollars marked down from — let's see — from $120, which includes the leather seats cleaned and treated, as well as the floor mats."

I ponder the price, wondering how much I might save if I do the job myself. But I don't ponder for long.

"OK. Let's do it."

"You got it, lady."

"How long will this big detail job take?"

"You got an hour to look at our 'treasures' in the gift shop," he chuckles.

An hour is a luxury to read, to write, perchance to dream. I relinquish keys, pay plenty for the big detail job, and drift to the gift shop laden with Christmas trees and ornaments, a confrontation that reminds me to polish off my Halloween candy.

I sigh and find cushioned comfort on the front porch of the faux Victorian building. I sit in full view of an ornate, two-tiered water fountain splashing in a gracious pool surrounded by ferns, a posh place to ponder while one's auto is in the salon.

How many thousands of people take notice of what's around them while waiting for their rigs to be reborn in sparkling metal splendor? How do they spend the time before glimpsing their clean Cadillacs, beaming Beamers, or scrubbed Saturns? Do they get the speedy express wash with their coupons instead of this big deal that I'm getting?

Stinging water hits metal, wet rags fly through the air in exchange for dry ones, and men shout orders as they dart among vehicles and compete with the drone of traffic on the expressway. In spite of machinery din and exhaust fumes, I am at peace in the crush of cars and people. I've read some poetry and recorded my thoughts, and I feel virtuous about taking care of my Toyota. I linger on the plastic wicker couch like an expectant grandmother in the waiting room, eager to glimpse the newborn vehicle. I'm excited to see what it will look like and what other auto in the family it might resemble — now that it's clean.

Christmas Joy

Yesterday was Christmas and, in the Bay Area of California, it was almost like spring. My youngest son, his wife, and their three-year-old daughter, Layna, took me to the cemetery to place Christmas flowers on Denny's grave. It was my second Christmas without him and a melancholy feeling had started to creep up on me.

But it didn't last long. The minute my young granddaughter stepped through the front door, she babbled incessantly about her presents, which snapped me out of my wistful mood instantly. In one long-winded, exuberant sentence, she announced, "Nonnie, Nonnie, I got a WHOLE BUNCH OF 'AMINALS' [arms spread wide] and a real KITCHEN THAT MAKES NOISES [palms up] and a car that MOVES [hands whoosh by] when I press the switch up and down [fingers wiggle] and we've got BEE-YOO-FI-DUL flowers for PAPA [slight pause, eyebrows raised] . . . he's not here?"

"No, Layna. Papa is in heaven, remember?"

She didn't bother to reply. Instead, she zoomed into the kitchen to find her parents meticulously molding four aluminum foil vases that would each hold a red rose for Denny's grave. When they were finished, we piled into the car and headed for Meditation Garden where Papa is buried.

As soon as she was strapped into her car seat, Layna declared, with the clout of a job foreman, "We need to yell REAL LOUD and tell Papa to get out of heaven and come to his house." She was so enthusiastic that her parents felt a need to shush her before we got out of the car.

Once we were at "Papa's house," we placed our rose-filled vases by his crypt on the bottom row next to the grass. My son knelt quietly to place his, and the rest of us followed his lead. Layna squatted near the ground, peered at the small rectangles, and whispered "Where is Papa's name?" I could feel tears welling in my throat. We pointed out his name and her tiny fingers touched each raised letter as she spelled "Papa" aloud. Then she shifted her attention to a brass name plate near her grandfather's and asked, "What does THIS one say?" It was a welcome distraction from the fragile emotions that we adults were attempting to conceal. Layna didn't stop until we had read the name on every brass plate near Denny's. Her curiosity lifted my spirits immensely and seemed to warm the cool air around us. Layna was intent on knowing who Papa's neighbors were, but she especially liked reading the letters that stood for people's names.

It surprises me that Layna still remembers her grandpa. My little granddaughter celebrated her second birthday only a few days after Denny died. Of course, my children have photos of Layna and Denny displayed all around their house, and she frequently points and says, "That's Papa." When she sees the support bars in our shower she always reminds us, "Those are for Papa." My family talks freely about Denny, so she is constantly reminded of him. But her recollections may be ones created by us and not her.

Whatever the source of Layna's memories, it was a delightful experience being with her yesterday at her Papa's new home. She was impressed with the oceans of poinsettias and Christmas trees of all sizes placed near graves and crypts. As Layna went about the business of righting tiny decorated trees that had fallen over, she chattered continuously until she was riveted by a family burning incense in a small metal box with fragrant smoke billowing forth. She had nothing at all to say about it. She simply stared for a long time.

By the time we left Memorial Park, she was exhausted and so were we. But Layna's enthusiasm was infectious and put us all in a good mood. We decided to go home and fire up the barbecue. It was, after all, Christmas in California.

Millennium

I had finally gotten used to the word *millennium* in everyday conversation when the phrase *Y2K* entered the scene. It had a catchy sound and look, but no one knew how long it took me to figure out what it meant. I was alone, thank God, when I realized it meant "Year Two Thousand." I said aloud to myself, "Oh, yeah. I get it."

The new phrase was plastered everywhere in big, colorful letters. It began to worry me. One night, a newscaster asked from the television screen, "Are you Y2K compliant?" I grabbed a strand of hair, twisted it in my fingers, and whimpered, "I don't know."

Media coverage made matters worse. It warned of problems with bank account numbers, documents, and records because of snags involving zeros and the number nine. It was far too complex to understand, and I had no idea what to do about it. I only knew that I wasn't prepared. Should I stash some cash, fill my tank with gas, and have plenty of food, water, medical supplies, and maybe a flashlight available? I expected looting and vandalism. My garage was too full of junk to make room for my car, so I worried that it could be in big trouble, unprotected in the driveway. It felt like the end of the world was coming.

The foreboding news of possible vandalism and looting filled me with dread, and I felt more alone than ever in my new role as a widow. It did not help matters that I would enter the year 2000 alone, without Denny beside me. He had planned a milestone celebration because the century would change on the heels of our fiftieth anniversary. It was a wonderful coincidence — but it wasn't meant to be. Denny had a date with cancer instead.

I declined New Year's Eve parties to stay home and guard my house and car — and watch the world fall apart on television from the safety of my bed. I felt weepy as I crawled beneath the down comforter alone and thought of Denny.

The television coverage was magnificent as it showed New Year celebrations and pageantry around the world. I was glad to see the mayhem hadn't yet started in other countries, but maybe only America expected chaos.

As I flipped from channel to channel watching the nations of the world enter the new century, I forgot to worry. Soon, I was too weary to witness the arrival of the year 2000 on TV, so I turned out the light and hunkered under the covers. I prayed that my street would be the same in the morning and my car would remain in the driveway unharmed. I was so tired from fretting that I easily fell asleep.

I had slept less than an hour when I was awakened by the sound of corn popping. I sat upright with eyes bulging. Had revelers invaded my kitchen? I picked up the phone to call for help and noticed the time. It was 12:05 A.M. New Year's Day. I cautiously peeked out the window. My car was still there. No one was in the streets. No lions or tigers or bears or *anything*.

Hearing the faint sound of firecrackers in the distance, I was reassured the house had not been overtaken by corn-popping prowlers. I said aloud, "Is that all there is? Where is everybody?" I had expected more in the way of celebration and hell-raising for a new century. I was so relieved. My whole body felt different. I had come through the front door of the Year Two Thousand alone and unharmed. I felt like Wonder Woman.

I crawled back under the comfort of down, fell asleep, and dreamed. I was ready for Y2K. *Anything* was now possible.

January 19, 2000

I finally took time to prepare a decent meal — a gourmet supper of scrambled eggs, green salad, toast with honey, and a glass of white wine. It was an odd combination, but it looked good to me. I had also assembled everything I needed to start a fire in the hearth. Sweeping a match across the emery strip on the box gave me a power surge of pleasure. The flame touched the crumpled newspapers, then flared up and shared itself with the kindling. What a satisfying sensation, knowing that I could still build a good fire! I took pleasure in the ambience I had created and enjoyed every morsel of my unusual dinner alone near the fireplace in my cozy family room.

The blaze soon spread to everything on the grate: cardboard, wood scraps, and two skinny logs. It crackled, spit, and spread a warm glow in the room. The fire was magical, casting a quiet spell over me that I hadn't felt for two years. Tina, my dog, was curled in her blanket on her new chair (my old chair) while I stretched out in Denny's recliner with my feet up. I settled in to watch a rented video.

Then I remembered — tomorrow would have been Denny's birthday. I sucked in my breath and tears leaked from my eyes, but I didn't interrupt my movie watching. In spite of the tears, I felt genuinely peaceful in my new chair, Denny's old one.

Soon the movie hooked me. Cate Blanchett was playing Elizabeth the Queen. After many youthful love affairs, it was pretty obvious that Elizabeth wasn't tending to the more important affairs of the country. She fought to stay in charge and got pretty mad at the men in her life. The beautiful young queen eventually had a temper tantrum that set the whole palace astir. She finally gained control by making a bold visual statement — she shaved her long hair to the scalp and painted her face white — to be sure she wouldn't attract any more men. With the unappealing look complete, she parted her pale lips and pronounced, "I need no man; I am married to England." From then on, Liz ruled the realm with confidence; she became a tough lady with no birthdays to remember.

Who was she kidding?

Conversation with Jane

BETTY: You know what, Jane?

JANE: What?

BETTY: If we did everything we are urged to do each and every day to maintain our female health and well-being, we might never make it out of the house!

JANE: Such as . . . ?

BETTY: Well, such as: brush teeth for two minutes or more; floss diligently; cleanse your face with cream, not soap; apply sunscreen; take hormone replacement therapy; do strength, flexibility, and cardiovascular exercises; do one hundred Kegel exercises; use eye moisturizer drops; take vitamins;

drink eight glasses of water; eat plenty of fiber and vegetables; eat a low-fat diet; practice visualization techniques to realize your fullest potential; practice relaxation, meditation, or yoga; and get seven to eight hours of sleep each night after brushing your teeth again and taking your nighttime medications.

JANE: And we'd still die.

Part 4: *Moving On*

The Orchard

Our family has lived near the apricot orchard for thirty-three years. Every spring the bare black trunks and branches of those squatty trees against an ocean of yellow mustard took my breath away. What a sight! Traffic slowed just to soak up the view. It was common to see mustard gatherers there, as well as amateur and professional photographers. One spring, the local newspaper even printed a half-page color photo of this spectacle, accompanied by culinary tips for cooking the mustard leaves.

But that was years ago. The once productive orchard, now neglected and ailing, is being forced to make room for progress. "3–5 BEDROOM, 2-½ BATH HOMES" proclaims the big, bad sign.

The planned removal of this historic grove created neighborhood outrage. It resulted in heaps of publicity, public hearings, anger, tears, and lots of petition signing. In the end, the apricot grove lost. Its wood is diseased, dying, and can't be saved — but big pieces of it can be.

At the edge of my driveway is a heap of rotten, termite-ridden, sawed-up chunks of tree trunks and branches. It's the result of a full day of physical labor by my son and his wife in order to salvage something from their past. The two of them sawed and loaded as much timber as possible into their pickup. My daughter-in-law wept as they labored. She had grown up near this place.

But what a mess! I couldn't visualize anything hopeful for this pathetic pile of solid sawdust, except the fireplace. But what do I know?

My son, the wood turner, had a plan. He introduced each piece to the lathe. I watched his chisel peel away layer after layer of the rough bark. The surface became smoother. Strange shapes and textures appeared, changed, and became new designs. Lacy holes and irregular openings slowly formed alongside other evolving patterns. The wood seemed alive. It was hypnotic to watch.

Weeks pass and the woodpile in the driveway is only slightly smaller, but my son has created beautiful containers of all sizes and shapes. Some have lids, and others have natural, irregular holes, cracks, and crevices — evidence of the maladies that probably afflicted the entire grove.

My wood turner and his wife displayed these newly created works on special shelves in their home. Some will become gifts for worthy people who must be informed that these containers are naturally fragile and ill suited for utilitarian purposes. They are objects of art and not meant to hold apples, nuts, beans, or even balls of cotton. They are already filled to the brim with memories.

My brother-in-law, a minister, admired the bowls along with the rest of us. He said that this kind of transformation reminded him of the first verse of an old, old church hymn. He recited it for us:

Dear Lord, take up the tangled strands
where we have wrought in vain,
That by the power of Thy dear hand,
some beauty may remain.

I like that verse a lot. Who would ever have guessed that such derelict-looking stuff held such latent beauty? It's as though the history of its splendor had been condensed into the rot, just waiting to be brought back for another shot at glory. May the orchard be with you, now and forevermore.

Flower Garden Fiasco

The garden beckoned, and the warm days reminded me that two seasons had passed since I last touched my plants. I've ignored the roses, hydrangeas, and pansies and stayed inside to write away my pain. I forgot the joy of planting, but then I remembered that I loved grooming old plants and pampering new ones. My garden flourished two springs ago when I lived all day in blue jeans and sweat. It felt so good to get my hands dirty and pull weeds again in the loamy, wormy soil.

For the second week in a row, I got up before the sun to work on my new flower garden near the street. It promised to be a glorious site if it ever got planted. First I needed to dig deep holes and remove large rocks. Then I would amend the gooey clay soil with gypsum and compost.

I had purchased $350 worth of plants and soil amendments the week before, thinking I would pop everything into the ground in one day. Little did I know that it would take three weeks before my beautiful flowers could set their hairy feet in soil. I hadn't expected my flower garden to be so much work! I struggled with two tasks: (1) to keep the one-gallon containers moist in a shady place while I prepared the ground for planting and (2) to keep my spirits up. Both were labor intensive, but necessary before anything pretty could bloom.

I became the curiosity of the neighborhood. Joggers stopped and asked why it was taking so long. Jokingly, I replied, "Because you're not helping me dig." Drivers slowed their cars and cautiously inquired, "Still at it?" My answer was always the same. "Yep, still at it." Most people watched from a distance after the first week.

What kept me going was my vision of sweet baby's breath, dusty miller, feverfew, alstroemeria, statice, and penstemon in fluffy masses in front of my sun-bleached, split-rail fence. The fragrant flowers and foliage would be dotted with white, silvery gray, lime green, pink, and purple. I didn't know until later that none of those flowers had any fragrance at all.

Very early one morning during the second week of work, I assembled my rake, shovel, plants, and kneepads. I placed my portable phone in a padded paper bag with handles so I could relocate it as I moved along the wide planting bed. In the street gutter I set six one-gallon cans of tall, graceful penstemon plants.

I proceeded to dig more deep holes and remove huge rocks each time my shovel clanged against them. The neighborhood was quiet except for the sound of my shovel when it hit stone and the laughter of three men at the top of the hill. They wore dark uniforms, and their fire engine was parked nearby. They were preoccupied with the hydrant at the top of the street.

While on my hands and knees, I was struggling to remove another small boulder when I heard the sound of gushing water. I looked up and was shocked to see a small wave washing down the gutter straight at me. I jumped up to avoid getting wet before I realized how fast it was coming. Then I remembered my six one-gallon cans of penstemon in the gutter along with my phone in its flimsy paper bag.

In an instant, the torrent of water claimed all seven containers, and they flew past me. The plants jockeyed for first position in this wet race toward the bottom of the hill. Tall penstemon was in the lead, with short penstemon in second place, and phone-in-bag in third. The remaining four plants bobbed and wobbled at an incredible speed, trying to catch up. I had never seen one-gallon plants go that fast.

Why in the world I yelled, "HOLD IT!" I'll never know. Maybe I thought the plants would obey me and stop in their tracks. I ran as fast as a mature person could go, grabbed the handles of phone-in-bag first, and tossed it onto my neighbor's lawn just in time to see the bottom of the sack break and my wet phone land on the grass. I continued to splash awkwardly in and out of the fast-moving water like an out-of-shape banshee, grabbing each gallon can of penstemon by the rim and tossing it out of the deluge of water. Miraculously, the plants and I landed upright. My chest heaved, but I was more concerned about phone-out-of-bag than about the plants, so I slogged back up the hill and retrieved it first.

As I dried off the phone with the tail of my dirty T-shirt, one of the firemen sprinted to my aid. Apparently he had heard me scream, "HOLD IT!" at the racing flowers. The closer he got the more anxious he looked. "Are you all right?" he panted. "We didn't expect anyone on the street this early. We should have looked before letting the dam break."

He asked, "What can I do to help?" I considered asking him to dig the rest of the holes for me, but I lost my nerve. Instead, I said, "If you could collect my runaway plants and bring them back alive, I would surely appreciate it."

As he went to their rescue, I took a few minutes to catch my breath and pull myself together. It was not the time to lose my cool. I still had lots of work ahead of me. The fireman clutched the six wayward plants in both hands as he trudged toward me and asked innocently, "Where would you like me to put these?"

I paused for a moment then replied, "Anywhere but the gutter."

The Carpet Man

In the middle of home improvements I had dashed to the rug mart wearing grubby work clothes, old sneakers, and no lipstick. The man who waited on me was a nice-looking guy with slightly gray curly hair, twinkling eyes, and a laugh like jazzy music. I had so much fun with him that I began to consider more than just a rug for my home. After that first meeting, I smiled all the way home and resolved to look better the next time I sought his advice.

I sought his advice the very next day, but this time I dressed for the occasion, complete with bright red toenails, a toe ring, and my best-looking sandals. To bring attention to my foot as we studied rug samples, I tapped it on the floor and gushed, "Now THAT'S a nice lookin' rug."

I discussed flooring with him often and became known as "his" customer. As his customer, I started wearing eye makeup and nice clothes, but I was still self-conscious about the wattle under my chin. It made me look old. If he stood to my left, I would hold my left hand casually under my chin to hide my wattle. If he stood to my right, I hid it with my right hand. It was a lot of work and, for the first time in my life, I considered having that wattle removed. I made a mental note to do some research in the yellow pages.

One time I called to say, "Carpet Man, I'm going to be gone for seven days, but I'll see you next week." He was in a goofy mood and affected an exaggerated southern accent, saying, "Betty, ahm so sahrry that y'all won't be comin' in today. Ah was so lookin' forward to seein' y'all. Mah heart will jus' be pinin' for ya 'til next week." That silly southern accent got me so excited that I considered carpeting the garage, the driveway, and the sidewalk.

I had never in my life had a harebrained flirtation like that, but it made me feel alive again. I was like a sixteen-year-old girl and all because of a guy who laughed a lot. We laughed so much that I was afraid he might get in trouble. "Carpet Man, your boss is going to think we're crazy," I cautioned. With a wave of his hand he said, "Hey, we're consenting adults over twenty-one and can do what we want."

Consenting adults over twenty-one? Thank goodness his ring finger was bare. It meant I could flirt forever. If he had asked me out for coffee — or even mud wrestling — I was so smitten that I would have gone in a minute.

But nothing like that ever happened.

I was busy for twelve months upgrading one floor after another. Everything was looking better because of my crush on the carpet man. I bought all new brass floor vents and carpeted the hall, stairs, and master bedroom. I had every scrap of carpet bound and had to hunt for places to use all those little rugs. I replaced the vinyl in three bathrooms and took out a home improvement loan to upgrade the kitchen so I could have laminate flooring installed. I stalked the carpet man for a whole year, but we never even went out for coffee because the only thing in my home that got his attention was the floor.

I'm not sorry. Apparently his "real" job was to open my heart, and he certainly did that. After the carpet man, I was ready to live and love again. And my house has never looked better.

Patchwork Dream

I spent a few days at my daughter's home, and the first night we talked about dreams. Renee said she dreamed of her dad almost nightly, and he was not sick, but alive, well, and normal. It made her feel happy. I had very few dreams I remembered and rarely one of Denny. Perhaps talking about them is why I finally had one that I could remember.

Unrelated events drifted through my head to come together in the same dream. First, I was disappointed at forgetting to watch Part I of Bill Moyers' documentary about death and dying, which he and his wife had worked on for three years. Second, I had also been thinking of Denny more frequently, which surprised me. Whenever I had a question, I instinctively thought, "I'll ask Denny" before I remembered that he was gone. Each time that happened, I felt lonesome. Third, I was preoccupied with the delightful man at the carpet store — a manager who helped me with floor-covering purchases for my home improvement projects.

My odd dream took place in a decrepit old building that looked like a remnant from a war zone. The setting was surreal in its decay. Denny and I wandered through the remains of the shaky structure and looked for some-one to join us on our inspection. That someone turned out to be Bill Moyers, with dark hair instead of gray. He was expecting us. The three of us had a huge job ahead. We were responsible for supervising the renovation. Bill Moyers and I did most of the work, discussing what each room needed as we took notes and acted important. Denny came along, but made no comment. We assumed that he agreed with all of our decisions because he smiled a lot.

Bill Moyers came upon a peephole in the middle of a large, undam-aged wall and peered through. "Hmm," he said. "This is odd. Come have a look." Denny and I peeked through the small viewing lens. The corner of the building had been damaged by an airplane and was left with a splintered framework of broken windows and concrete. Through the fractured remains of the walls, a single empty window frame stood erect. It encompassed the late afternoon of the metropolitan skyline in a stunning formal balance of classical beauty. It reminded me of an ancient Greek composition like those in my art history books.

A wall had been built to isolate that damaged and broken corner to avoid the cost of rebuilding it. As we gazed at the view of the city skyline through broken walls, we could see the old linoleum on the floor covered with a thick, moist layer of fine, dark dirt. The dirt was the finest compost I had ever seen, and we agreed it was worth saving even if we didn't bother to salvage anything else.

I finally asked Bill how he knew Denny, and he said, "I used to be his secretary." That was strange. I thought I knew all of Denny's secretaries be-fore he died, and I wondered if this were heaven. But I knew Bill Moyers was still alive and that I had missed Part I of his TV special on death and dying.

I continued with Bill and Denny, as we made the rounds of the decaying site. It took all day, and we barely made a dent in our inspection. It grew dark and we were tired, so we decided we must spend the night in the building and resume our work early in the morning. But, first, we needed to find two bedrooms that remained intact. I looked forward to snuggling against Denny whether he talked or not. We finally found one bedroom with a double bed that actually had a couple of blankets and two pillows — but nothing else. The three of us squeezed into it like spoons pressed snugly together. Denny was behind me, Bill Moyers was in front of me, and I was in the middle with my head in the crack between the two pillows. Before I dozed off, I rubbed Bill Moyers' upper arm the way I used to rub Denny's arm before he fell asleep. We were tired, but cozy, as we three "spoons" slept in that huddled position.

It was comforting. I thought of how lonely it had been in my big house and queen-sized bed, and there I was, protected by two men — one in front of me and the other behind me in a little double bed with two pillows and two blankets.

The next morning I awoke alone under the covers in my daughter's guest bed, wondering where my two guardians had gone. I closed my eyes again and replayed the "dream disc" in my head as though it were a movie. The dream had a lot of meaning for me. The remains of the weakened structure seemed to be my life after Denny's death. Bill Moyers was my "guide" through the wilderness of widowhood, while Denny was, and always will be, a mute presence in my life. The carpet man, although not even a bit player, probably provided the materials to help put the devastation back in order.

With my thoughts sorted out, I stretched, threw back the covers, and put on my robe and slippers. I was ready to join the family for coffee and toast because I had a dream to share.

Lonesome

My neighbors are dear and so are my pen pals. I'm with a lot of people from time to time. The carpet man's attention resurrected my heart, but I'm lonesome.

I see other writers about once a month, and I share intimate humor with my luncheon crones. The women in my swim class have become treasured friends, but I'm still lonesome.

I see my sons weekly. I write to my daughters, and I hug my grandchildren whenever I can. I love their dear faces and cherish their existence while I'm lonesome.

I love my computer because it's my confidante, but whenever I say so it doesn't say it back. I hug my friends' husbands, and they don't seem to mind because they hug me back. Some are poor huggers so I volunteer to teach them because I'm lonesome.

I watch tender movies about people in love, and it fills me with longing and makes my eyes water. Someday I'll find my own place in this world, but for now I'm just lonesome.

The Night that Lizzie Got Baptized

It was the second time in my life that I had taken part in a Catholic mass, and the place was packed. I was to witness my nineteen-year-old granddaughter's initiation into the Catholic community. Lizzie was one of fifteen adults who would be baptized and confirmed and then receive the Eucharist. A godparent and a sponsor accompanied each one of them. Our family, her dad's family, and her friends joined the entire parish community to celebrate the vigil for Easter.

A priest joked with the congregation by saying, "I see that several of you have brought your sleeping bags again this year." My son Bob and I didn't get it, so my daughter enlightened us. "That means we're going to be here for a looong time," she said with a sigh.

It was, indeed, an endless ritual. I embraced the service more than Bob did since he had pulled weeds all day and arrived depleted. His job that night was to keep five-year-old Layna, my youngest granddaughter, from getting restless. Armed with crayons and a coloring book, Layna was a jewel, but her daddy was already falling asleep.

Working up to the initiation of those fifteen was like the first scene of a three-act play. It was an event of its own. Respectful and patient attention was paid to scripture reading, singing, and making declarations of faith. A great deal of time was devoted to each portion of the liturgy and, after an hour had passed, things finally seemed to be winding down. Layna's daddy looked grateful, and he started putting away the crayons. Then the priest, trying to be humorous again, announced, "Folks, you'll be happy to know that we are now one-third of the way through our program."

Bob's eyes glazed in disbelief and he mouthed the words, Oh my God. "DADDY, YOU SAID A BAD WORD!" Layna said in a loud whisper. In disgust, she turned to her cousin and said, "Nathan, my daddy said a bad word." Nathan and Bob shushed her while I grabbed my mouth and pushed back the giggles.

But we pulled ourselves together, and the pace . . . inched . . . forward. After much singing, chanting, kneeling, standing up, sitting down, and praying, there was also some holy water sprinkling, lighting and blowing out of candles, anointing, and blessing. The event ended at 10 P.M. Lizzie, with holy water in her hair and chrism oil on her forehead, was in rapture as she marched out with the others to a grand organ processional with four priests trailing behind.

But, it wasn't over yet. We still had photos to snap of Lizzie with her dad and their family, Lizzie with our family, and Lizzie with our two families together. We had grown sick of the word "cheese" when one of the boys said, "What does cheese say when it has *its* picture taken?" We then took photos of those goofy kids doubled over in laughter. Do you get the picture? We did. LOTS of them!

Photos finished, we gulped our pink punch, gobbled egg-shaped Easter cookies from Safeway, hugged and said goodbye to all relatives, dumped Layna into her car seat, and pointed the Toyota for home. Bob pleaded, "Don't invite me next year." In spite of my numb butt and aching back, I couldn't stop thinking about the night.

Many things helped me embrace the event. Nathan, my eleven-year-old grandson, sat next to me when we sang, and I cherished the sound of his astonishingly sweet voice, thinking to myself, "He's good." Hearing him switch back and forth from falsetto to the deep chest tone of a boy pleased me, because his rhythm and pitch were so accurate and his tone so clear. He even had a modest vibrato. I used to sing and wondered if my grandson was following in my footsteps. When Nathan grew weary, he put his arm around me and rested his head on my shoulder. I was enchanted by his voice, and I was in heaven with his gestures of affection.

During the long service I had felt moments of spiritual peace. And when Lizzie had faced the congregation, I was filled with awe at her youthful beauty. "When did she become a woman?" I wondered. My throat tightened and tears burned my eyes. It was a wondrous moment and a memorable day. I felt so blessed to have this family.

Confessions of an Addict

"My name is Betty, and I'm an e-mailaholic." That's what I'll say when I find a support group. An ugly word, *addiction*, but I fear that's what it is.

Three months ago, I joined an online writing group. This group of aspiring writers encouraged each other to write at least thirty minutes daily to keep up their creative energy. Finding thirty minutes a day to write was not my problem. Finding thirty minutes a day *not* to write was. Imagine what it's like now, three months later!

When I became active in my writing group, I stopped going to my daily exercise class. While my literary skills are improving, my body is losing the tone gained from months of water aerobics. My children don't call me their "jock mother" anymore — a name I love and miss. Now, after sitting far too long at the computer, my body aches, and my house and yard are in complete disarray.

The time had come to break this cycle of endless reading and writing e-mail, so yesterday I made a commitment to return to water aerobics. I gathered my equipment and laid my bathing suit by the bed. Tomorrow I would *not* go downstairs in my housecoat and open my e-mail. Instead, I would dress in my bathing suit and go to the eight o'clock class. With enthusiasm for my journey toward recovery, I set the alarm.

The alarm rang at seven-fifteen the next morning. I shut it off. The sight of my bathing suit on the chair made me ill. How could I have thought I would actually jump out of bed, put on that bathing suit, and drive two miles to get wet? I must have been crazy. I skipped the eight o'clock class, staying in bed to wrestle with my conscience instead.

I finally put on the suit, feeling cold and uncomfortable, and forced myself to drive to the nine-thirty class. Too many people greeted me upon my arrival, saying they'd missed me and asking where I had been. I didn't dare tell them I had returned to class to put an addiction behind me, start my life over, and get myself back in "jock" mode. Instead, I said, "I simply got sidetracked, [Charming laugh] but I'm back for good." I tried hard to believe it.

A new instructor led the class, a strong-voiced, young, tan, athletic chick. The workout was a killer. I had forgotten my water bottle. My body felt bad. I couldn't see straight. I was terribly out of shape from sitting in one place for three months in front of the computer screen. I faked my way through and felt better for it, but only in my head.

This was a good lesson for me, as it would help me see the error of my unhealthy ways. With only one class under my belt, I knew I was on my way to recovery. A great many thoughts ran through my mind between the pool and my car. It was not a long way, but it took a long time because I couldn't walk straight. While driving home, I resolved to change my habit of checking e-mail every hour.

I stumbled into the house as weak as a kitten and too weary to think. I moved in a daze, sat down in the desk chair in my wet bathing suit, and stared at the blank screen. I had barely enough strength to reach for the mouse and raise my shaky forefinger to click. I stayed there until my bathing suit was dry.

The Conference

I was not a writer when my husband was alive; I became one after his death. For two years I wrote about life with Denny, and I wrote even more about life without him. Everyone loved my stories — so much that they said I should publish them. I agreed and signed up for my first writer's conference to find an agent. I was so naïve.

Four years earlier, I had attended a function at the same conference grounds in the small coastal town of Pacific Grove, California. But I had never driven the winding mountain roads alone to get there. Barely freeway literate, I was so eager to find an agent and get published that I became Wonder Woman with a car. I filled the tank with gas, memorized the directions, and headed for the highway.

Two hours later, and after missing a few turns, I finally reached my destination. I inhaled the fishy air and savored the fragrance of cypress, expecting good things to happen here. After claiming my fat registration packet, I checked into my assigned room. The simple furnishings and the spare, institutional environment suited my purpose. It was a serious, no-frills arrangement — no TV, no phone, no room service, no maid. I was also treating myself to a private room because getting acquainted with a stranger was not an efficient use of my energy — and because I snore.

For the next three days, everything I heard about being published was news to me. I had no idea that becoming an author was so commercial! I had a lot to learn and for once, I listened more than I talked, taking notes I could barely read. One of the first things I scribbled in my spiral notebook was, "The writing business is glutted with new people who have NOT done their homework."

I would soon find out that I was one of those people. When I sat down with an agent for the first time to make a pitch, I didn't know the proper "pitch patter" and took too long gathering my thoughts. The agent interrupted with, "State quickly what you want to say." I cringed with embarrassment but attempted to pull it off in a few succinct sentences. In the middle of my anxious presentation, she frowned and broke in again with her curt business voice. "Do you have a proposal?" Of course I didn't, so it was pretty clear that my turn at her table was over. I felt so foolish, a widow who thought she was a writer.

All I wanted was a crumb of encouragement from somebody in this business, so I licked my wounds, pulled myself together, and chose an agent at a different table only because she smiled all the time. I waited in line and when it was my turn, she smiled while informing me there was no market for my kinds of stories. "However," she continued, "that would not keep me from looking at your work if there was something unique about it." I told her that I hadn't yet discovered what was unique about my writing, but she handed me her card anyway. It made it easier to climb out of the hole of self-pity.

I had hoped to hire an agent, but what I needed even more was to get some validation that my writing was worthy of publication. I wanted audience approval, so I decided to go to Open Mike Night to share one of my stories. Each participant was allowed only three minutes, and the word was out that long-winded readers would be stopped in the middle of a paragraph. I didn't like the sound of that, so I found a three-minute story and timed myself repeatedly so I could safely finish before the bell. I told the guy with the timer to relax — his work was done.

I read "Confessions of an Addict," a good choice since the moderators and the small, intimate audience laughed in all the right places. What a rush that was! They referred to me as "Erma Bombeck with heart," calling my anecdote "inspirational" — the kind of writing that appears in newspaper columns every week. They said, "Your stories are probably ready to go if you can find a paper that will carry them. You don't need an agent for that."

I had been put on the bench, but Open Mike Night got me back in the game.

The next person who met with me, Bruce, my seminar advisor, had already read thirty pages of my stories before the conference. He, too, suggested they were like columns or articles. During my seminar meetings he said many things, but the most important was, "Betty, you're a wonderful writer." He said it twice. I counted. Bruce said that in order to get my collection of stories published, something was needed to make them different from the other memoir books on the market.

He also suggested that I leave out my poems, which disappointed me. He felt that the mainstream reader does not access poetry well — even poetry like mine, which anybody could understand. He also urged me to continue writing stories and assemble far more than I needed for one book. And even though I had no title yet, he came up with a subtitle: *Recipes, Maps, and Stories.* The word *recipes* didn't feel right because it sounded like a cookbook, but I liked the reference to a map for a good reason.

I found my way to the conference with a map that Denny had high-lighted several years ago for a different occasion. The night before I left on my quest for publication I was desperate for directions and rummaged franti-cally through the jumble of carelessly folded papers in a box labeled "MAPS." I finally found the one I was looking for and opened the untidy bundle on the kitchen table. As I flattened the creases with my hands, I was stunned to see Denny's meticulously drawn, neon-yellow pen line showing me the way. He provided for me when he was alive and continued to do so after he was gone.

On the second anniversary of his death, Denny's map had shown me the way to my first writers' conference. The event was a defining moment condensed to a weekend. It was inspiring, emotional, exhausting, and eu-phoric, and I looked forward to doing it again. But the next time I go to a writers' conference, I'll do my homework before I leave — not after I arrive.

Inheritance from Allie Belle

Today a friend in Oregon invited me to stay with her family and speak to her women's group, a professional gathering called the *Tigard Business Women's Forum*. Jan said, "We've been talking about nothing but business, and it's time for something light, inspiring, and humorous. Can you read your sto-ries and tell us why you gave up art for writing?"

"You won't have to ask me twice," was my immediate response. I shared this exciting news with my best friend, Connie, and she said, "You do know who's living vicariously through you, don't you?"

I was blank. I had no idea.

"Your grandmother."

"Oh, my gosh. You're right."

I keep forgetting about my grandmother's life *before* she became my grandmother. She was a dynamic force in my childhood, but during my mother's childhood she was a public speaker. A poster from the early 1900s advertised her program as "entertainment for the whole family."

My grandmother was born Susan Alvina Elarton, but it didn't suit her as a proper stage name. While still in high school in Independence, Iowa, she was already planning a career in front of an audience. Elocution was her favorite subject. So my grandmother legally changed her name to Allie Belle before she even graduated from the twelfth grade. The month after gradua-tion, she married her shy, redheaded sweetheart, Elmer Eastburn, and they started a family. But motherhood and housewifely duties would not get in the way of her dream of being on stage. After all, she hadn't changed her name for nothing.

Allie Belle Eastburn was a radically religious woman and a zealot about the path one must follow to ascend to the pearly gates and sit at the right hand of God. She tolerated nothing of a worldly nature from her three children. That included card playing, movies, or anything under the big tent of Barnum & Bailey. So the children enjoyed their pleasures in secret. My mother once knelt at the side of her bed to ask God's permission for a fun day at the circus. Since she was certain that the Almighty would not answer the way she hoped, she prayed to the devil instead. As soon as her frolic at the circus was behind her, Mom returned to her bedside, knelt again, and asked God for mercy.

"It was the only way I could have any fun when I was a kid," my mother told me.

Allie was what, in these modern times, would be called a "groupie." She loved the atmosphere of the big tent revival meetings so popular in the Bible Belt in the early 1900s. Eventually, she signed on with the Chattauqua movement's public speaking circuit, which brought culture, medicine shows, and revival meetings to the rural folk of the Midwest. Although unordained, Allie Belle preached sermons at revival meetings along with her other gig: speaking for the Women's Christian Temperance Union.

The WCTU was a radical anti-liquor organization. Their primary goal was to bust up taverns with axes. But my grandmother disagreed with Carrie Nation's way of putting things right. She felt that too much energy was wasted in breaking things. My grandmother's "target" was not the beer joints, but the children. Allie Belle felt that drunken behavior could be prevented before a child ever tasted liquor. Her method was to rent a meeting hall and give families a lively program (so said the poster) that included anecdotes from the Bible and enticement for the children to come up to the stage and sign a pledge stating, "My lips will never touch the demon alcohol." My grandmother's fervor was driven by the fact that her three brothers were wild, rowdy railroaders who got drunk every weekend.

Many of Allie's weekends were spent giving lively presentations advertised as "Never a Dull Moment...All Work Original." To make these programs appealing for little ones, Allie Belle sometimes dressed as Mother Goose. In one of the picture postcards that advertised her local program, Allie, decked out in costume, sits on the ground surrounded by kiddies from the audience along with her own three children (my mother and her siblings) who were wearing expressions of boredom and disgust.

Eventually, Allie's offspring grew weary of the "show" and wanted out. Surprisingly, my grandmother agreed to let her kids retire from the stage. But each time she had a public-speaking tour scheduled, she left them at home to take care of each other. My mother remembered those days well and told the following story:

When I was twelve, my father and we three kids were on our own because Mama had left us for a two-week speaking engagement on the road. We didn't do so well while she was away. We fought over who would prepare food and do the chores. My father was so gentle and sweet that he didn't know how to handle us. He left for his railroad job each day never knowing what kind of mess would greet him when he returned home. He was sick of it. We were sick of it. As mean as Mama was, she was the one who ran things and we all did what we were told, even our father. When she left, we fell apart. My father decided to make the point with our mother that she was needed at home. So he lined up all the dirty dishes from the front door to the kitchen sink. We three kids didn't think it was a wise thing to do, but it was my father's passive way of protesting.

When Mama returned from the circuit tour, she opened the front door expecting to see a tidy home. Instead, she saw all those crusty pots, pans, and plates, and she was livid. In a rage, she flung her suitcase against the wall, making a hole in the plaster, and started kicking the dishes with both feet until everything glass was broken to shards. Mama's kick was so powerful that she limped for a week. My father and we three kids were left with a terrible mess to clean up.

Three years later my grandparents divorced, which was also not common in 1921. My mother and her mother were not like other mothers and grandmothers. They were not the cookie-baking sweeties that you see in books and movies. They were passionate, dramatic, and volatile. They yelled, screamed, and threw things. They were mean and couldn't stay married.

So now that I'm trying my hand at public speaking, I've been reminded that it's my heritage. It skipped my mother, who was a gifted pianist and musician, and landed on me instead. If I had to inherit something, I'm glad it was my affinity for the stage and not a less admirable quality.

All of my life, I have vehemently denied any similarity to the women in my family by saying, "No way in hell am I anything like my mother or my grandmother." But perhaps I am. They were both creative spirits and loved to perform. They inhabit my spirit and are alive in me. But I don't break dishes — that practice stopped with my own mother. And I stayed married to the same man for forty-nine years.

The Love Goddess from Los Gatos

Before my first-ever presentation in Tigard, Oregon, one of the women introduced herself by saying, "Hi, I'm Tammy. I hear you're from Los Gatos?"

"Oh, yeah," I said. "How did you know?"

"It says so right here in your program," she responded.

I laughed at myself because I thought she had said, "I hear you're the Love Goddess," and I was having fun with her by agreeing. I imagine my new business card reading:

> *Betty Auchard*
> *Writer, Speaker,*
> *Love Goddess from Los Gatos*

I like it.

Too Much To Do

I wish I didn't feel duty-bound to keep my home in topnotch condition. It's made me a prisoner. I'm afraid to let things go. If something is broken, I hire a stranger to fix it as soon as possible — and there's always something broken.

It's important that my yard stay beautiful because it's my way of saying, "I'm still here and I can do it on my own. I don't have to move to a retirement community just because I'm single and seventy." But it's no easy task.

For example, it's taken a long time to find tradesmen I trust, filtering out the flaky ones and keeping the best. Neighbors ask, "Betty, who cleans your gutters, trims your trees, and fixes your plumbing?" They think I know what I'm doing just because my husband did. Maintaining Denny's standards while following my own creative path is sometimes more than I can manage.

The time it takes to find good workers and hover while they work is time I need for writing. And writing seems more important than home maintenance. People might never forget my stories, but I doubt that they will remember me because my plumbing was in such good condition or because my grass was always mowed.

I don't want to look down from heaven someday and hear, "Gracie, do you remember Betty Auchard? She was the woman up the street whose windows were so clean that you could see everything that went on in that house." And Gracie will say, "Oh, I'll *never* forget those windows."

I've considered letting the maintenance slide so I can get a whole book written, but I've seen those houses with weedy lawns, broken blinds, and raggedy curtains hanging in tatters at grimy windows. Sometimes there's a pale old person peering out between the shreds. I don't want that to happen to my home or to me.

I want my home to look warm and inviting. I want my neighbors to reflect on my memory with fondness when they say, "I remember Betty. She's the one whose house looked simply 'mahvelous' from the street, whose books of stories were memorable, and who had an affair with a great guy. Was it our mailman?"

Yep. That's what I really want, *all of it: a super boyfriend, a writing career, a well-kept home, and a lawn that gets mowed once a week. It's a lot to do.*

I'm New

Two of my good friends have just lost their husbands. I'm watching them wade through the deep waters of grief, which will someday grow shallow and will not be as dark and turbulent as they are now. Sometimes I dip my big toe in the same familiar, liquid darkness, but it's not as frightening as it was. Since Denny died, I've learned how to swim.

In my first written works, over three years ago, I often opened with humor and closed with grief. I bounced from laughter to tears and back again whenever I wrote about the strange new world of a widow — my world. It was a confusing, sad, and funny place to live. But I soon learned the language, the gestures, and the deep breaths one must take to keep a tight throat from turning eyes to water in an instant.

But that is now history. My new life is good and sometimes better than ever before. So I share it on paper in case I forget what it was like. When I'm not writing, I'm going places. I fill my own empty gas tank to go to the movies with Lorraine or spend an afternoon of delights at the deli with Alice.

In my future, there might even be a fun evening with a guy named Greg, whoever he might be. I wonder what he's like? He might be waiting in Gilroy for my grief to go aground, not knowing that it did a year ago. Most of it is now a memory that pressed stories from my heart, stories that opened with humor and closed with grief. Now earthly pleasures and places are teasing me, filling my heart with hope. I'm feeling alive again.

Part 5: *The New Me*

Lookin' Good

*I*had just gotten over a yearlong crush on my carpet man, who was fifteen years younger than I and thought of me only as "the most fun customer he'd ever had." Of course, he never actually "had" me in the carnal sense; he only sold me rugs. In spite of my disappointment, I held no grudge, for the carpet man did me a huge favor. He opened my lonesome heart and placed inside it a longing to love again. My job was to stitch it back together and keep that longing in place. My life would never be the same and I had to get used to it. In fact, my future could be anything I wanted, and I wanted it to be remarkable. I wanted to live fully, embracing the future on my own terms, and I didn't want to miss out on anything tantalizing that came my way.

But I also wanted to look good when it did.

So, five days a week, I divided my time between swimming laps and working out in a health club. I experienced an endorphin high like I'd never felt before and found pleasure in humble tasks like doing the dishes and cleaning the toilets.

My spirit became vital, and my body grew strong. I lost twenty pounds. I was a jock who smiled a lot because *most* of me was lookin' good. But, sadly, my face and neck resembled the drapery department at Sears. I was truly dismayed. I felt more youthful and energetic than ever before in my life, but my face didn't match my spirit. No exercise in the world was going to rid me of all that loose skin. As I fingered the flaps of floppy flesh on my cheeks and under my chin, my Spirit spoke to me.

"Betty, behold! You need a face-lift."

"Oh, but that's foolish!"

She replied, "Go, my child and do foolish things — but do them with enthusiasm."

"Oh, man." I whined.

"No dear. I am a woman. One more thing, Betty — you never know when your second act is coming, so you'd better be ready for it."

Now I'm a spiritual person, but I considered that the voice might NOT have been Spirit, but Vanity instead. I liked the possibility of having smoother cheeks and eyes that showed for a change. And with my wattle in a wastebasket instead of on my neck, I would be able to hold up my chin without hiding it with my hand.

My future looked good and, soon, so would I.

I decided to take Spirit's advice and go for it. I gathered all the necessary paperwork and broke the speed limit getting to my bank to take out a home equity loan. The loan officer said, "Have a seat. How much do you want?"

"Oh, whatever I need to upgrade my . . . uh . . . kitchen."

"Good for you. We encourage people to maintain their personal property."

"Oh, I couldn't agree with you more. It will increase my market value over the long haul, right?"

"Right. I can see that you've done your homework, Mrs. Auchard."

"Oh, yes — I have." (If he only knew.)

He whisked out the papers, asked questions, filled in the blanks, summarized the details, and finally said, "OK, dear, sign by the yellow X."

I knew this might change my life, and I smiled all the way home.

I don't recall parking the car, but I do remember sprinting into the house in search of the yellow pages. As I pondered the listings for "Plastic Surgery," visions of vinyl implants and razor-sharp tools gave me the willies. The phrase "Cosmetic Enhancement," however, appealed to me. It had a softer, more user-friendly sound. So I took a deep breath, licked my finger and, with anticipation, turned the pages toward the Cs.

Betty Gets Pampered

Patty worked with my cosmetic surgeon to prepare patients like me for a face-lift. She taught me how to take better care of my skin, so I could protect my investment after the surgery, and how to use salves and ointments on the skin that was to be laser-treated. She provided super-strength sunscreen and medical makeup that would cover the red, bruised places around my eyes, cheeks, and neck so I could go out in public before the scars were healed. In addition, I was getting what Patty called "the works," which was on the house. Although she probably did this for all her pre-surgery clients, I got the feeling that I was being treated as a special customer.

I had never had a facial and "the works" involved more than I expected. Patty fastened a small towel around my hair and gently cleansed my skin with potions that smelled pure and clean. For about thirty minutes, she sanded my face with microscopic crystals, running a miniature, hand-held vacuum cleaner along my cheeks, forehead, chin, and neck. After she was finished, Patty placed a mirror in my hand and said, "Have a look. Can you see the difference?"

"I can't see much because I'm not wearing my glasses," I replied. "But I can *feel* the difference." My face was warm, like peach-colored velvet, and I imagined that I glowed.

She then used a portable machine to infuse oxygen into my newly sanded skin. It was like standing in a cool breeze on a mountaintop. Next, she packed my face with slime, which for some odd reason I imagined was green, and placed cool, damp gauze over my eyelids. Finally, Patty tucked more warm towels around the edges of my whole body, turned down the lights, and left the room. For ten minutes, I relaxed in luxurious comfort while hypnotic music played on low volume.

I was euphoric. I felt so nurtured and at peace that I lay there and let a wave of emotion carry me up and away — and I wept. I'm sure it had something to do with having recently passed the three-year anniversary of Denny's death and feeling grateful that I was finally moving on. But it was also the pure bliss of being nurtured instead of being the one who did the nurturing.

When my aesthetician returned, I sniffled, "Patty, while you were gone, I relaxed to the meditation music and cried with pure joy." Putting my emotions into words caused me to sob again. The moment affected Patty, too. She was so touched that she put her head next to my cheek, gave me a hug, and wept with me.

That night, I drove to my writer's club meeting feeling rested and content. In the midst of crushing traffic, I heard cars honking at each other like angry geese. But I was removed from it all, floating above the stresses of other drivers like a beautiful cloud. I felt smoothed-out everywhere, not only on my face but in my soul. I traveled the freeway with a peaceful expression on my face and a smile on my lips. At the meeting, people said nice things to me such as, "You look pretty tonight ..." and "That color looks good on you ..." and "You must have been in the sun today because you're glowing."

I glowed because I had found a source of untapped energy and was radiating an inner light. I was becoming a new woman.

Pondering My Future

Young people think the future is a long way off, and middle-aged people are planning for it. But I'm beyond those age groups, so I think about it all the time. I wish that I didn't.

I count the number of years I may have left, and they seem short. So I want to be all I can be, and I don't want to waste any of it on self-defeating behavior or meaningless activity. I also have a lofty late-life goal, and that is to be a published author.

The fact that I can do anything that I want because I'm a widow sounds good to some women, but it has its drawbacks. First of all, I'm now a person run amuck, with an unorthodox schedule. I eat cookies with cold milk when I'm hungry, write until sunup, and sleep when I get tired. When in a marathon writing mode, I don't get dressed. When the day is over, I just put on a different nightgown before going to bed again.

The most frightening freedom is spending money without negotiation — but what a rush! I've upgraded my home way beyond our master plan, which has greatly reduced my reserves, but the place looks great.

Having my wattle — that hangy-down thing under the chin that makes one appear older than she is — removed reduced my financial reserves even more. But I hated it and who needs money anyway? I wanted to look good in the waning years of my life, even if I had to pay for it, so I said, "Wattle, you're goin' down!"

I have other goals, as well. I plan to stay fit for life because I feel better and because I like being the oldest woman who swims forty-two laps at the pool. I must always hold back enough money to take a trip whenever I want, and I'm determined to stay in my large two-story home until I'm carried out. I will keep my front yard beautiful, and if I can't do it myself, I'll pay for a real gardener, not just a guy who mows the lawn. I shall clean the house for myself and not because someone is coming to visit. And each day I hope to get organized and pay the bills on time.

I intend to have my life stories read from a book someday instead of through e-mail, and I would like, always, to be good company. And even though I'm over seventy, I'm not old, so I'll keep wearing what suits me: sweatshirts, blue jeans, and sneakers.

I long to meet a nice man. We could hang out together and hug. I might meet a hugger at the senior center if I renew my membership. But I don't like being reminded that I'm a senior. Most of all, I want to take things as they come and regret nothing that I've done. I make every day count, just as my mother did. She once said, "I want my money and my breath to run out at the same time — with nothing left over."

I rarely agreed with Mom on anything, but I agree with her on that.

The Big Dance

The other widow in my neighborhood went with me to the big dance last night — but barely. Her heart wasn't in it. I pushed her.

"I have nothing to wear," she whined. But she did and I knew it. "I'm paralyzed at the thought of it. I'm not sure what to expect."

"Well, Wanda, if you're not comfortable, we can leave. Who needs to have a good time?"

As for me, I wouldn't have missed the dance at our local health club. I was willing to go alone. And my determination was probably the push that Wanda needed, though she complained that she didn't really know how to dance. I said, "Nobody knows how to dance these days. They just writhe and wiggle to the beat and *call* it dancing."

If the truth were known, I was just as nervous as Wanda. But I didn't want to miss any chance to mingle that came my way. Lowered inhibitions and the beat of foot-tapping music were two of the best ways I knew to make new friends. I wanted to mix with people who were health nuts and kept their bodies in good shape. I had joined them and the human race again quite some time ago, and I wasn't going to remain under the gloomy cloud of widowhood any longer just 'cuz I didn't have a date.

So my friend and I squeezed into our best clothes and slapped on our makeup. We looked pretty nice, but looking good didn't hide Wanda's anxiety. I wasn't suffering from self-doubt; swimming laps at the pool had improved my body as much as my attitude. I *was* apprehensive that I might dance with such abandon that I would make a fool of myself, because I love to dance. I mean I *really* love to dance.

By the time we arrived, the place had been transformed from a health club to a dance club. Cloth-covered poolside tables lined the deck, and lights cast a romantic glow over everything. Black and silver balloons arched over the swimming pool and covered the ceiling of the lobby. Wine was being served, and the tables were laden with the most inviting morsels I had seen in a long time.

The place was packed with suntanned, robust health club members of all ages. The men were dressed in dark suits and the women in glitzy strapless gowns, so Wanda and I didn't exactly blend in. But as I introduced her around, I could tell that she was beginning to relax. We armed ourselves with glasses of white wine, filled our paper plates with gourmet goodies, and found a table with two empty seats where people welcomed us.

As we got acquainted with the couples at our table, we found we had many things in common. By the time we had emptied our plates, our little group felt so warm and fuzzy-friendly that we exchanged e-mail addresses and promised to write.

But as much as I enjoyed the friendliness of strangers, I could no longer ignore the foot-stomping music on the dance floor. It was calling to me, but it didn't seem to be calling to Wanda. Reluctantly, she joined me in a crowd of couples who felt the beat and a need to express it. I felt the same need and wondered how long I could hold out with Wanda not even tapping her toes.

We found a table right under the nostrils of the band. But Wanda wanted to move — too loud for her, just right for me. We relocated to the back near the door for easy escape in case she couldn't stand it anymore.

It wasn't long before I *had* to do my own thing, but I didn't do it straight down the middle. I did it in the wee, narrow borders at the edges of the dance floor because there wasn't much room and because I didn't care. The beat in my bones just needed to escape and reveal itself, and where it escaped wasn't important. Other single women felt the same, and they soon joined me as I bounced and shuffled to the rhythms in a tiny, squashed space at the edges of the music mainstream. In our excitement, we bumped into Wanda sitting in her chair. So we danced around her, holding out our hands, inviting her to join — and finally she did. She rose from her chair and kept time to the music. Wanda was groovin'.

But not like I was.

I danced with abandon. I had finally freed my spirit to express the tempo of my soul, and I was tireless for the rest of the evening. Every time I looked up, Wanda was still moving to the music with a small group of women at the edge of things. By now I was all over the place, straight down the middle and around the edges, weaving my way through couples who didn't seem to mind that I was doing it alone. Everybody was having a good time and being helped by a wild and wooly live band that never stopped playing.

For me it was far more than a good time. It was a primal dance of freedom announcing that I had joined the world again.

It was quite wonderful.

As I drove my friend home, then hugged her goodbye, we agreed that it was the most fun we'd had in a long time. Wanda's parting words were, "Betty, I'm glad that I went. You've introduced me to a whole new world. I wanna be a wild child like you."

That was the nicest thing Wanda could have said to me.

Sherry

For nearly three years, I'd been living in my huge home alone. My husband and I raised four children here, and I didn't want to leave it because I love it. But I'd lost my motivation for many things such as cooking for myself, paying bills on time, and keeping the roses alive. I forgot to feed the dog and failed to lock the house at night. I had no direction. But Sherry is changing all that.

Sherry has been my housemate for four months. Twenty-five years younger than I, she's a blonde hairdresser who calls herself a "cut and color girl." But she's more than that. She's a Vidal Sassoon-trained stylist who learned her skills in London. Her clients are devoted to her. Her friends are faithful and few, and I became one of them. Even my dog, Tina, prefers Sherry's company to mine because she's a woman who doesn't forget to feed a dog.

Though in her mid-forties, Sherry is a spontaneous young girl when she's in the mood for adventure. She took off with a friend recently on a freezing midnight trek to the mountains in hope of seeing a rare meteor shower. She's a unique breed of girl/woman, a Texas-grown original full of surprises.

She was born to parents who were still in high school and depended on Sherry's grandparents to raise her. When she was fourteen, her grandmother died, forcing Sherry to assume adult responsibilities, doing all the cooking, cleaning, and laundry while attending ninth grade classes. After a year as a widower, her lonely grandpa married a Cajun woman who was hot-tempered and cruel. She beat Grandpa and Sherry frequently, and both often nursed minor injuries. But a wound sustained above Sherry's right eye when her face was pushed into the corner of a door was the event that caused fifteen-year-old Sherry to leave home.

For the next two years, the gutsy girl managed on her own, but she had no time for the usual teenage distractions. Sherry was too busy holding down a job at Bally's gym in Dallas to pay the rent on a rat-infested apartment and attending high school as well as beauty school. She graduated from both during the same week.

Because of her strong will and stubborn disposition, Sherry learned at a tender age that she could depend on no one but herself. The burdens carried when she was a teenager have shaped Sherry's adult attitudes about all things. She is efficient. She doesn't waste time on pretentious jabber, and she strips language of its jargon. Her philosophy in life is simple: The bottom line is — if you want something done right, do it yourself or forget about it.

This morning, I heard a shriek from her bedroom.

"MY GOD! CAN YOU HEAR IT?" she bellowed from her end of the hall.

"Hear WHAT?" I yelled from my bedroom on the opposite side of the house.

"IT SOUNDS LIKE A SCENE FROM *FARGO* OUTSIDE," she told the whole neighborhood.

I put my ear to the air and caught the harsh grinding of wood in a chipper. I had to admit that it did sound like the grisly scene in the film where evidence of a murder was being destroyed. A short time later, I heard her rupture with laughter as she dashed to the bathroom for a drink of water, choking on her own sense of humor.

"WHAT'S HAPPENING NOW?" I yelled.

She was breathless and shrieked, "You should SEE some of the men being sent to me by this DATING service."

So I hiked down the hall to her room and had a look. She stabbed a finger toward the computer and said, "Just look at this dude on my screen!"

I contemplated the strong-framed, slightly gray-haired fellow dressed in kilts and holding a bagpipe. I thought he looked kind of nice and asked, "Sherry, what's wrong with him?"

"An old guy with a bagpipe? Are you KIDDING? I'm only forty-six years old." The bagpipe guy never had a chance. Sherry deleted him and rushed on to other hopefuls sent to her by the matchmaking service. The next candidate sent a dramatic letter. Sherry read it aloud with theatrics, her hands clutched to her bosom.

"Lady, your photo is bee-yew-tee-ful. I love your cheeks, your chin, your nose, and especially your sunglasses. Where did you get them? I am pretty good lookin' myself so open my photo with caution, because you might find just what you're lookin' for. P.S. I am a red-hot lover. Signed, RRRrrrrrraahmon."

Sherry rolled the *R* in Ramon's name with such noisy display that it reduced both of us to giggles. As she auditioned each candidate on the screen, she conversed with their photos, making comments like, "Hey, dude, get rid of that mustache and I *might* think about it," or "Whoa, guy! Who cuts *your* hair?" I had to lean against the wall for support while laughing. We carried on like that through an entire list of dating candidates. By the end, I was hoarse.

Sherry Berry, as I call her, has put my house in order because she knows how to do it, but she watchdogs *everything*. One day she said to me, "Why did you put that salt shaker there?"

"Because there was an empty spot."

"It doesn't go there. It belongs over here."

"Oh. OK."

I give her free reign to organize my cupboards because she cares and I don't. She buys the groceries and cooks the food. We eat well because she prefers organically grown produce and meat with no chemicals. There is always something wholesome prepared and just waiting to be eaten. We are never out of food. I don't exist on cookies and milk anymore.

But worldly and wonderful Sherry has a different personality from mine. Compared to her, I might appear passive when watching world events on television. I absorb the bad news of the day by pondering it before responding to it. But Sherry's reaction is immediate. She might shout at the screen, "OH, MY GOD. George Bush is out of his MIND, if he has one!"

She is occasionally my mother and always my friend, giving me advice regarding my lack of a love life though she has none of her own. She says, "I'm on a sabbatical from love by choice, so for now, I'm just speaking from experience." We're basically two women without men, but she behaves as though she doesn't need one.

She brims with self-confidence when she says to the television screen, "News lady, your hair is all wrong and so is your makeup. You need my help." But she instills self-esteem in others with statements like, "Honey, you've got the perfect butt for those pants."

Sherry has integrity. She knows what's considered good or bad taste and shares her knowledge with clients. One day she dealt with a new customer who wore that "short in front, long in back" haircut made popular by Billy Ray Cyrus. Sherry calls the style a BIFPIB, which stands for "business in front, party in back." The drop-in client didn't know it, but she was about to be educated.

Sherry said thoughtfully, with arms folded across her chest, "There is a name for your haircut. It's called a mullet, and this is a mullet-free zone. We *fix* mullets here." And she showed the woman a book that made fun of the dated hairstyle.

The woman said, "Why can't you just take my money and do what I want?"

Sherry took a calming breath and proceeded. "You know why? If you leave this salon with a mullet that I trim and other mullet-heads ask where you had your mullet maintained and you told them, my reputation would be ruined. I couldn't sleep at night and I would have to move to another city. I don't do mullets."

The woman was so stunned that she couldn't speak. Before she left, she turned to have one more look at the Texas blonde who refused to trim a mullet.

But Sherry can be softhearted and generous. She will cover a bounced check until an out-of-work client can repay her and she often carries the burden of others. She helps her family financially, but woe to the guy who does her wrong, for her wrath is quick and razor sharp. She dealt harshly with a boyfriend who showed up at her shop to freeload. "Oohh, now I see what you had in mind, lover-boy. You just wanted a free haircut. Well, I'll give you a free haircut," she said as she picked up her scissors, "but you won't be able to go out in public without your hat."

She's tough as tires, but she can cry herself to sleep when hurt by a lover or a friend. I know. I can hear her down the hall.

The difference in our ages does not alter our ability to communicate. We're like two girls in a dormitory. We can spend a whole evening talking about men, because we love them and miss them. We found each other out of need. She needed affordable housing, and I wanted to stay in my large home after my husband died. We give a lot to each other. She's got a home, I'm still in mine, and neither of us is alone anymore.

The Day the Ants Died

The rain was merciless and had driven ants into every corner of the house. We were learning how to live with them. But I couldn't tell Sherry, my housemate, how much food I'd thrown away because there were dead ants in the boxes. If Sherry knew about this, she would eat nothing from the pantry until we cleaned it out.

Why aren't they alive, I wondered? And what killed them? The ants were probably in danger of drowning outside in the rain and came inside to keep warm and dry in the powdered sugar. Maybe they died of suffocation.

I don't care *where* ants meet their maker, but I don't like them on the menu. One morning I almost put their crinkled bodies on top of cinnamon rolls that I had made for Sherry. She would have asked, "What are these black specks in the frosting?" Nothing gets by her.

If that had happened, I would have said, with my eyes closed as if deep in thought, "Um, let's see. Was it Julia Childs who suggested a pinch of pepper in frosting?"

"Is she NUTS?" Sherry might ask with her nose all wrinkled and her eyebrows arched as though she smelled a rat.

"Well, Julia said it's like yin and yang for the taste buds — peppery vs. sweet."

I would have rolled that lofty lie off my tongue as though I believed it myself because I wasn't prepared to empty the pantry. I had a pile of other things to do, and finding which cartons contained ant bodies was not on my list. So what if we accidentally ate a dozen dead ants? There must be some protein in their tiny bodies. It wouldn't kill us.

At least . . . I didn't think it would.

I had convinced myself that the ant problem was temporary and assumed that I would discover any new black specks before Sherry did, so I put out traps called Ant Motels and read the instructions again:

This formula attracts ants. The traps are safe to place in your cupboards. Do not spray or disturb the trail. Several traps should be located where ants are entering the house. Within three to five days, the ants will disappear. They will all carry the secret ingredient back to the colony and all of them will die.

That wasn't the most comforting information I'd ever read. But neither Sherry nor I met the same fate as the ants, so the secret ingredient must be lethal only to bugs. On the other hand, maybe we just didn't eat enough of them.

Stickers

My sixteen-year-old grandson, Danny, helped load stuff into my car trunk so he, his mom, and I could take a weekend trip. Before he climbed into the back seat, he asked, "Nonnie, where's your sticker?"

"Sticker? What sticker?"

"Your car registration sticker for this year."

"What is a car registration sticker?" I asked.

That was when I started learning from my grandkids. Danny, who had never even cared about riding a bicycle when Denny was alive, knew all about the DMV because he was in driver's education classes in high school. When I found out how to get my car registration sticker for that year, I also found out that I was eight months past the due date. It was just another one of Denny's jobs that was now mine. So I pasted the new sticker on top of the old sticker four months before the next one was due to be paid.

It seems that I would have learned my lesson, but I didn't.

Four years later, my car (with no current registration sticker displayed) sat in the Oakland Airport for two days. It was an easy target for a citation. Imagine the rookie cop's delight when he said, "Gotcha — only thirteen more citations to go," and then added another notch to his belt. I could just picture him scribbling out ticket number seventeen and thrusting it under my windshield wiper blade while his eyes swept across the lot for citation number eighteen. Our cars were sitting ducks in the long-term parking lot.

Getting the citation really bummed me out. When I returned from my trip, I had felt empowered for having found my own way in and out of a major terminal while it was undergoing construction. But finding a citation under my windshield wipers turned me into a whiny victim. I soon learned that the fine for having a poor memory was $60.

After that, whenever I got a feeling of self-assurance and started patting myself on the back for all that I'd learned in over four years of widowhood, I stopped to look around. Self-assurance was a sure sign that a new screw-up was waiting to happen. Forgetfulness kept me edgy, which made it hard to relax. And repeating the same mistakes definitely eroded my self-confidence. For nine months I had been breaking the law. However, I was sure I had paid the registration fee this time. I knew I would have to track down the problem the very next day, but I had no idea where to start. Before going to bed, I downed two glasses of merlot.

I slept well that night, getting up at 7:30 to fix hot chocolate laced with coffee and Irish Crème. Then I read the paper, pretending that it was just another day. After reading the paper, I finally had to get real. I pulled my thoughts together and forced myself to relax. Of course it didn't work because *force* and *relax* are not compatible. I knew all along that I was destined to spend the day with the DMV. I kept thinking, "What to do, what to do before I call the DMV to be put on hold for twenty minutes?" I decided I could postpone the phone call by going through my files first. I drained my coffee-laced chocolate and liquor, took a deep breath, and dived in.

An exhaustive search of my records used up an hour, but it revealed that I had, indeed, paid my car registration. But where was the sticker? Anxiety was starting to do its dirty work. After another hour, I found that I had neatly filed the envelope hiding the sticker with the receipts for paid bills. With that discovery and the release of tension, I felt twenty pounds lighter. I hugged the envelope to my chest, closed my eyes, and paced the office repeating, "Oh, thank you, God. Thank you, God. Thank you, God!"

I dashed to the garage and stuck the shiny new sticker on top of the dirty old one. In spite of the fact that I was nine months late displaying the sticker, and $60 poorer, I was charged with enthusiasm for turning another page in my life. I promised to become a better car owner next year. And since next year's responsibility was only three months away, I looked forward to getting that burden off my shoulders as well.

But I couldn't help asking myself, "Sheesh . . . what's next?"

My Controversial Christmas Tree

Three weeks before Christmas, I browsed through the Crate and Barrel catalogue for new ornaments, tree skirts, and garlands. They were so gorgeous that I longed to buy them. New holiday trimmings might help me get in the mood for decorating. I had never enjoyed decorating a package, a room, or a tree of any kind. Part of my lackluster attitude about embellishment was the temporary nature of the activity — so much work to be enjoyed for such a short time. But now visions of new Christmas décor danced like sugarplum fairies in my head.

I easily convinced my daughter-in-law, the original shopper, to accompany me to the huge Crate and Barrel store in the new upscale mall. We wasted no time. We drove, we parked, and we shopped, scooping up one satin tree skirt, two velvet pillows, three chains of garland, and a basketful of red and gold balls.

The next stop was a downscale mall to purchase new lights. The choices were many: transparent, opaque, tiny, large, green, white, purple, and red. I voted for tiny red lights and a shiny gold ball to crown the top of the tree. I could hardly wait to start dressing it.

Excitement overtook me as I wound five boxes of red lights from the top to the bottom of my Christmas tree. By the time it was laden with red and gold baubles, my enthusiasm had become my passion. I couldn't believe how intensely I enjoyed beautifying the tree. That evening, to get the full effect, I turned off all but the tree lights so the only thing visible in the room was a glowing red triangle. It was spectacular.

I stepped outside into the cold night air, then to the middle of the street to view it from a short distance, and then from my neighbor's front yard across the street. My red tree in the window was breathtaking. It was especially dramatic compared to the white lights that glittered from every other neighbor's window. I was so excited that I didn't mind shivering as I admired the spectacle from the street. I pondered singing the *Hallelujah Chorus* and anticipated wholehearted admiration for my distinctive tree. Instead, the responses were varied and emotional:

"It's so red."

"I LOVE IT! It's romantic and sensuous."

To be honest, your tree wigged me out."

"It's warm and inviting."

"It's out of place and doesn't fit."

"It makes me feel good."

"It's a cross between beautiful and scary."

"Is it radioactive?"

There wasn't a single neutral comment. One person asked, "Doesn't it bother you that your tree has generated so much controversy?"

"Not at all," I insisted. "I love the attention my crimson tree has created." It was the truth. Finally, I cared about a Christmas tree like I had never cared for one before. And I intended to defend my creation against those who didn't appreciate that it was just a little bit different from other holiday trees. I liked being near it. During the day, I turned on the red lights and curled in an overstuffed chair near its branches to sort through junk mail. At night, I sat across from its warm glow in the darkened living room and listened to Christmas carols. I dreaded the time to dismantle it because I would miss my new friend.

Proof of my fondness for the bright red thing came when I opened a gift from my daughter-in-law, the "born-again shopper." Inside the bag were five new red and gold ornaments to add to the others we had just purchased. I was so touched by her gift that my eyes watered. It was like giving birth to my first baby and receiving gifts of clothing to cover its nakedness.

After the New Year, I'll undress the tree. But I'll not toss the new adornments into any old box. I plan to store them in their original packages with such care that they will look just as nice next year as they do now. And perhaps the dissenters will adjust to the smoldering radiance of my holiday tree. Eventually they will realize that I intend to defend those scarlet globes until they burn out — and I will replace them when that happens. The red Christmas tree lights are here to stay. I glow just thinking about them.

Boy George Took My Picture Today

George is a very young guy who likes to skateboard in empty swimming pools. He has a thick, wild ponytail that cascades down his back and jeans that rest loosely a couple of inches below the waistband of his denim-colored underwear. He was also my photographer. "Boy George" takes pictures for the *Los Gatos Weekly* and the *Saratoga Times* newspapers.

According to George, the article that was to accompany my photograph had already been written. It was in recognition of the Steinbeck Centennial — and that's where I came in. As a writer, I was active in that celebration. George was to get a good photo of me that *might* be on the cover of the *Los Gatos Weekly*. I was dumbfounded.

"On the *cover*? Why me?" I asked.

"Because you're a Los Gatos resident," he replied, "and when a member of the community is involved in something newsworthy, like the Traveling Steinbeckian Readers, the newspaper lets the neighbors know."

So George came to my home and took gazillions of digital portraits of me holding "Steinbecky" props like the *Grapes of Wrath*. As a model, I tried for two hours to feel natural as I smiled for George's camera. He took so many pictures of me pretending to read without my glasses that I felt like a literary Cindy Crawford. Then George narrowed his eyes at a little screen on the back of his camera and said, "I think you need more lipstick."

I was horrified that I had set my lipstick down when George rang the doorbell. All of those photos were wasted! But George said, "Not a problem. We have a lot more pictures to take." The plan was to take more portraits of me reading the *Grapes of Wrath* in front of the author's former residence on Greenwood Lane. We unfolded a map to locate the address and set off for the hills of Saratoga.

As a journalist's helper, I tried approaching a man working in the yard. "Sir, may we take a few pictures of John Steinbeck's former home?"

The guy didn't even look up as he replied, "I'm installing an electric fence to keep Steinbeck groupies like you off the property."

"OK. 'Bye." I was a little embarrassed.

As a result of being turned away, George and I had to go back outside the gate, where he took photos of me leaning casually against one of Steinbeck's trees. With some effort, I found an unbumpy spot. I hugged the

Grapes of Wrath against my chest and smiled at George's forehead and one eye, for that was all I could see of him from behind his camera.

Then, just for fun, I suggested that he take a photo of me peeking through the wide openings of the fence at the Steinbeck home below. The book cover was still showing in my arms, but I was peering through the fence like a voyeur when George said, "Betty, I don't want the back of your head. Turn your face toward me and smile that great smile." So I beamed like a flashlight as he snapped exposures one after the other. We both laughed, and he said, "After all this effort taking a 'good' portrait of you, the paper will probably use one of these silly ones."

"I hope not," I replied. "I want to look as good as I can in case a nice retired man with literary interests seeks me out because of your great photograph."

George's laughter tumbled from him easily. We drove down the narrow road and into another driveway where we could turn our cars around. It was an abandoned view lot for sale. In spite of the panorama, the property was weedy and unattractive, a bit on the raspy side. The house was gone and all that remained was a lean-to shed and an empty swimming pool.

Something grabbed George's attention and he dashed down the steep hill toward the pool. I assumed that he had found another photo opportunity for the Steinbeck property from a different angle, so I propped the *Grapes of Wrath* in my arms for another portrait. I heard him shout, "I wonder if I could skateboard in this empty pool." When he got close to the edge of the kidney-shaped cement hole, his shoulders sagged. "Oh, no. It's full of rain water," he said. With some difficulty, I imagined this tall photographer skateboarding up the sides of an empty swimming pool with his ponytail flapping behind him and his denim-colored underwear peeking out the top of his jeans.

As he wrapped up the photo shoot, he gave me a hug before I even asked for one. His embrace was a "shoulders-touching" hug, stiff and self-conscious. But I resisted my usual response whenever I get a humble hug from a man, which is, "You need hug lessons, and I'm just the person to give them."

George waited for me to navigate up the steep driveway and then he turned his car around to lead me out of the Saratoga Hills. I followed him down Highway 9 until he changed lanes to go his own way. When I punched my horn to say "goodbye," he tossed a smile and waved.

I was excited at the thought that my photo might be on the front page of the newspaper, but I'm glad I didn't spread the word around until I saw it for myself. My photo was buried so deep inside the article on page sixteen that most people never saw it. On the cover was a pencil drawing of John Steinbeck scowling at whoever was drawing him. He wasn't as lucky as I had been. He wouldn't have been scowling if Boy George had taken his picture.

Part 6: *Ready for Romance*

One Half of a Couple

*W*idowhood is an isolating experience. When I lost my partner, I lost my social life, as well. Couples won't ask singles to dinner unless they come in pairs. So neighbors never know what to do with me except chat on the grass and ask, "How're things going?" or to say, "Wow — look at you. You're coming along fine."

"I am," I say. I'd like to add, "And thank you for noticing that I'm doing just fine by myself." But that sounds sort of snotty and self-serving, like a whiny-assed widow.

I've given this some thought, and I think that it's not their job to entertain me. It's my job. I must socialize myself.

I might do it this way: I'll ask a guy to pose as my beau. My neighbors wouldn't know that I bribed the postman to pretend that we're closer than anyone ever suspected. I'll invite the whole block to join in our fun, for we're throwing a potluck and asking *them to come — even the singles.*

I Want to Live

When Denny died, half of me went with him, and I wasn't sure if that part of me could ever be restored. Since I was the only one who knew that I wasn't all there, it appeared to others that I was handling the loss pretty well. My eyes were bright and slightly glazed, not from crying but from wondering what day it was and what I was supposed to do next. No one knew that I had to write everything down on a list so I wouldn't forget the most common tasks:

    1   Put garbage out Thursday night

2   Pay bills

3   Put gas in car

4   Find someone to show me how

And then I could never find the list.

People didn't know how many times I went through red lights. At social gatherings, others were mystified when my laughter suddenly turned to tears and then back to laughter. Eventually, I appeared to be my old self again, but I was the only one who knew that nothing was ever going to be the same. So I embraced the future, transforming as I moved forward and unsure of where I was going. And I did very well, but no matter how much I accomplished, I didn't feel complete. I longed to be a whole person.

That yearning to be whole is stronger now than it was four years ago. Something is still missing. I'm convinced it's the desire to love and be loved again. But I can't waste precious time while love is looking for me, so I'm cleaning house so there will be room for it when it arrives.

I've let go of much that I once treasured. I look at objects that I held dear and realize I can finally live without them. They're extra baggage, and I don't need them for this next trip, wherever it takes me. I value each day, accepting mortality. I'm ready for whatever crosses my path and will let nothing good pass me by.

I want no regrets when it's my turn to die.

The Man at the Lion's Club

I had been invited to tell my "surviving widowhood" stories to an audience of men. Even though I had always thought of my target audience as women, I must have been wrong because there I was making the presentation to the Lions Club, which was mostly a male audience. My apprehension evaporated when I saw that they were enjoying every word. As I shared my adventures and misadventures about learning how to be a single woman at the ripe age of sixty-eight, some of the men's faces wore an understanding expression and others shook their heads in agreement. The program was followed by enthusiastic applause from the audience of six women and thirty-four men. It was gratifying.

I relocated to the back of the room to sign books and CDs and to visit with the members. One man hung back as though he wanted to talk to me with no one else around. When the time was right, he approached and said, "I think you and I need to get together."

Omigosh. Was this nice-looking gentleman asking me out? I swallowed hard, placed my hand to my chest demurely, and managed to say, "Oh, really?" I was quite flattered.

"You and I need to get together and compare stories," he continued. I was puzzled. "We men go through the same thing that you women go through after your spouse dies," he explained. "My wife died a year ago and now I have to learn to feed myself."

"How are you doing?" I inquired.

"The first thing I attempted by myself," he said, "was breakfast in the microwave." I assumed he was cooking oatmeal. He continued, "I put four eggs in the microwave on high power for four minutes."

"Oh, no." I was aghast. "What happened?" I asked.

"They exploded." We both grimaced. "I could hardly scrape the eggs off the walls of the oven 'cuz they were just as petrified as I was."

His admission started a competition, and we tried to top each other. I told him that I hadn't known how to put gasoline in my car. He told me about the mysterious white stuff clinging to his freshly laundered blue jeans. I said that it was probably a tissue in a pocket. Then I told him about overpaying my bills because I didn't know what the minus sign by "amount due" meant. And he told me about doing laundry only when he had no clean shorts left in his bureau drawer.

What I'd thought was the senior citizen version of a pickup line turned out to be a legitimate sharing of stories. After comparing experiences, I considered adding a chapter to my book called "What Men Go Through." Research for the chapter would naturally place me in the company of a great many widowers with all kinds of stories to tell. What a sweet cover that would be for an eligible woman seeking male companionship. I could do research forever.

My Friend Barry

My friend Barry and I have many things in common. We both have a background in music, and our deceased spouses were both psychologists. We talk, take walks, and discuss our children and grandchildren. Barry and I read poetry aloud and love much of it, but don't understand all of it. We both get the giggles after two glasses of wine, and we enjoy each other's company. He admires my writing, and I appreciate his sense of humor. If we had met when younger, we might have gone steady or perhaps wed, but we didn't. We met when we were senior citizens seeking companionship instead of marriage.

Each of us is content in our own home, with our own routines, independent lifestyles, and friendships with other people. We're happy to have found each other and hope to stay close until one of us dies, becoming a sweet memory in the heart of the other.

Barry never knew my husband, though he's getting acquainted with him through my stories. Barry reads every one. That's a lot of stories! Barry is my number one fan and, occasionally, my critic. Once, when Barry was a passenger in my Toyota and telling me how to drive, I reminded him, "Hey, Barry — knock it off. You're reminding me of Denny."

He knew exactly what I was talking about and said, "Oh, please don't write a story about me after I die."

His remark made me smile, though the likelihood of Barry dying before me is strong. He battles fatigue from heart problems and sometimes I don't see him for several weeks.

One hot day, when my friend was relishing a cold beer while reading my newest creation, I interrupted to say, "Excuse me for a few minutes, Barry. It's time to close up the house." He was used to my doing that, but this time after I had shut every window, drawn all the blinds, and shut the doors in all eleven rooms, he asked, "How do you know when to close your house up to keep it cool?"

"When the outside temperature is the same as the inside."

"Did Denny teach you that?"

"Yes, he did."

"Do you continue to do it out of respect for his memory?"

"No, I do it because it works."

He smiled at my response and asked, "When do you open the house up again?"

"When I can't stand it anymore."

Barry asked if that was the way Denny did it, too. I told him that Denny and I never agreed on the right time to open the house. Denny was scientific about it, watching both the temperature and the clock. He cautioned, "It's possible to open the house too soon, and all our cool air will be out the windows."

"What cool air?" I usually protested. "I'm suffocating in here." I told Barry that's why I now open the windows when I feel like it.

Barry is beginning to know the habits I developed after living with my husband for almost forty-nine years. He has said more than once, "I think I would have liked Denny."

I always smile and respond, "I agree, Barry — and Denny would have liked you, too."

Boyfriend Report

I'm running out of room on my calendar for appointments. This happened because I joined three singles' groups at one time and then became a restaurant evaluator. My children constantly ask, "Mom, what's going on? You're never home anymore." I chuckle to myself, thinking, "Yeah, and it's about time."

Evaluating restaurants allows me to comfortably ask guys to go out with me. The corporation gives me two assignments each month and they suggest that I ask a companion to go along since two people are better than one. Cecil, a seventy-five-year-old widower, assisted me with one of my restaurant reviews. We dined at a very nice Italian place, and he was helpful in ways that I couldn't possibly evaluate. For instance, I sent Cecil to the "john" so he could tell me if it was clean and well supplied. He expressed disappointment that there was no urinal.

"I hate using a toilet seat in a men's room," he commented. "You never know who's been sittin' on it." True. But don't guys use those seat covers the way we girls do? I hated to ask, even though I'm getting to know Cecil pretty well.

Whenever Cecil picks me up for a date, he brings something good to eat because he likes to cook. Once he presented me with a loaf of homemade banana-oatmeal-pecan bread — deee-lectable. Another time it was pasta in tomato sauce and after that came eggplant relish, a blue-ribbon preparation. The night of the restaurant evaluation, he brought something for Tina — the food bowl that once belonged to his beloved, now deceased, dog "Muffie." What a sweet gesture!

After the wonderful dinner, we sat in his car while I made notes about the restaurant from his prompts and my memory. That done, I thought he might like to check out a place in the country that had live music and a small dance floor because Cecil said that he likes to dance. Well, he hemmed and hawed and said he wasn't too sure.

"But, Cece' I thought you were a dancing kinda guy," I said.

"Yeah," he replied, "I am, but what kind of music do they play at that place?"

He referred to it as "that place" because I had previously told him that on Sundays, it was a biker's bar. But this was Friday night and "that place" would be overrun with folks of all ages who loved to "get down." No motorcycles would be lining the parking lot, but cars would be packed into every available space at the Almaden Feed and Fuel located way out on a country road.

My answer to his question as to what kind of music they played was, "The loud and stompin' kind of music from a live band." That's when I lost him. Once he knew that the Almaden Feed and Fuel was a bump and grind, groovy atmosphere, he declined by saying, "Aw, Betty — that's not my idea of dancing when you can't hold your partner romantically in your arms." Cecil likes old-fashioned, smooth moves to good music from the forties. So I'm not sure that he and I will be spending much time doing the disco. But he likes to be with me because I make him laugh and forget his woes. He lost his wife only seven months ago.

Hank, sixty-six years old and very tall, is another new friend who also lost his wife seven months ago. He says, "Betty, you lift my spirits."

"That's nice to hear," I yell up to him since I am very short. His legs are so long that it's hard to keep up when we walk. Dancing with him is like being in a tornado — we cover a lot of territory in a very short time. I probably enjoy being with Hank because he's younger than all of us — my other boyfriends, their deceased wives, and me. But it rattled me that his departed wife's name was Muffie, also the name of Cecil's deceased dog.

Then there's eighty-two-year-old Seymour, who doesn't hear very well. We each lost our spouses five years ago and his late wife had the same interests that I have. She, too, was a writer and an artist. The first night I met him, he invited me back to his home to see her paintings.

"Mmm, I don't think so, Seymour," I replied. He was genuinely disappointed.

At the Mother's Day barbeque, where all the men treated the women like queens, I met a vital, spunky, white-haired widower named Rudy. He's fun, lively, and will *not* divulge his age. He said, "No matter what anyone says, once they know how old you are, they get a slight prejudice and define you by the years that you've stayed alive." Rudy could be a ninety-year-old stud for all I know. He's a member of my health club and plays tennis once a week.

One morning, I thought I saw Rudy at my gym. I approached and said, "Hi, Rudy." But it wasn't him. It was a man who could have been his twin. It confused me, but not as much as it did him. I explained to this complete stranger that he *must* meet my new friend because it was uncanny how much they resembled each other. Then this "new" old guy, who wears no wedding band, laughed and said, "Well, that's the cleverest pickup line I've ever gotten from a lady. My name is Ben. What's yours?" We now give each other a high five whenever we meet.

Since becoming a member of three groups of people without partners, I'm smack dab in the middle of an active social life with Cecil, Hank, Seymour, Rudy, Ben, and Ed, another brand new friend who's a lot of fun. And I don't want to forget about my buddy Basil. We used to see each other a lot, but now his energy is focused on staying well. He still gets in touch with me between chemotherapy treatments, but I miss our dinners together.

Although I enjoy all my boyfriends, the guy with whom I have the *most* fun will pick me up Friday for a picnic in the park where we plan to sketch. Bernie, my closest male friend, is gay. He's preparing the picnic in exchange for a drawing lesson, and I am just the person to teach him. But what he really wants, even more than drawing lessons, is an update on my social life.

Dear Matchmaking Service

Dear Online Matchmaking Service:

Attached is my photograph and profile; my handle will be "Spritely."

I'm a seventy-three-year-old widow of five years, far younger in body and spirit than my age would imply. I'm a spiritual person, not doctrinal, so I don't attend church. Whoever God might be, I pray to Her because I'm a creative agnostic.

I'm seeking companionship, not marriage (at least that's what I think), so I'm interested in a single man between the ages of sixty and seventy. Please don't send any men my age because they're usually too old for me. I want someone with a sense of humor who enjoys lively conversation, good books, films, and all kinds of music — not just the "olden goldies." A non-smoking, healthy fellow would be a bonus. Time is going by fast, so I look forward to hearing from a gentleman soon. I might add that I'm passionate about many things, especially dancing, and I would love to dance with a guy again. But it's not a high priority as I can always dance alone. — *Spritely*

ProseChild

Dear Spritely: A woman lovely as you should never dance alone. I'd love to have a note from you. — *ProseChild*

Dear ProseChild: But I do dance alone every morning in my nightgown to smooth jazz playing on the radio while the coffee is brewing. It's like going to church. — *Spritely*

Spritely, dear, you're a woman after my own heart. Tell me more about yourself.

Well, ProseChild — I'm writing a book.

What do you write about?

I write about the events of my life and the people who cause them. So tell me, P.C., what do you do?

Well, Darlin', I drill holes for gas and oil wells, but I repair old violins as a hobby.

Really?

Yes, really.

ProseChild, I used to play the violin.

Used to . . . ? Why did you give it up?

My precious old violin has come unglued and needs to be repaired.

Spritely, Darlin' — I can help you with that.

That would be wonderful, Prose.

Spritely . . . my name is Ray.

Nice to meet you, Ray. Call me Betty.

Betty, a violin is a terrible thing to waste. You should bring it back to life.

Ray, I don't even know where it is.

Betty, start searchin' for it today.

Ray, I promise to hunt high and low as soon as we get off the computer.

So . . . Betty . . . if you were to find your beloved instrument and I helped get it restored, is that what you would call an "event?"

Yes, indeed — a major event.

Betty, am I going to be in your book?

Well — I'm not sure, Ray. We've only just met.

Young Guy

DEAR GORGEOUS OLDER WOMAN: I am fifty-five, and you are just what I'm looking for. I am financially stable, divorced two years, and miss cuddling and kissing with a passionate lady. Would you consider a relationship? I can send a photo if looks are important. — *Young Guy*

DEAR YOUNG GUY: I'm flattered that a man your age would consider me as a (gulp) lover, but I'm afraid it would seem more like incest than a loving relationship. — *Spritely*

Spritely, I'm terribly disappointed. Could we at least be pen pals?

Of course we can, Young Guy. Tell me something about yourself.

�֍ �֍ ✖

Soulmate

DEAR SPRITELY: I have sent two "winks" your way and you haven't responded. What do I have to do to get your attention? — *Soulmate*

DEAR SOULMATE: I'm sorry that I didn't wink back, but you live so far away that I didn't want to encourage you. — *Spritely*

Spritely, we have so much in common that I think we should at least talk. I am a retired art professor who loves to dance. But I want to know why you gave up art for writing.

After the death of my husband, words and a keyboard took the place of brushes and paints and became my creative tool for healing. Now writing is my passion. Why do you ask?

Spritely, dear . . . I ask because I really think we could make beautiful art together. I have a huge studio on my property in the woods here in Alabama. And why don't you want to get married again?

Soulmate, I got married very young and have never been single before. I need to find out what it's like to be on my own before settling down.

Spritely, that's too bad because I'm looking for a wife, and you're a nice lady. But it was awfully nice talking with you.

❈ ❈ ❈

Cool Dude

DEAR SPRITELY: You're a sexy lady and I'm a sexy guy. We could keep each other company. I live fifteen miles from you, so how about it? When can we get it on? Maybe this weekend? — Cool Dude

DEAR DUDE: I'll tell you why we won't be "getting it on" this weekend. When a brand new gent comes into my life and the first thing he mentions is sex, it appears to me that all he has to offer is his skin. Make no mistake, I'm a sensual woman, but you and I are off to a bad start and would not be compatible. So let me end this communication before it starts! — Spritely

❈ ❈ ❈

xDrummer

HELLO, SPRITELY: I've been a widower for six years and I just joined this site a few weeks ago. We have things in common, such as a love for music, good books, and dancing, to name a few. And I have a reasonable sense of humor, I think. And surprise, surprise, we live in the same area. Shall we chat? — *xDrummer*

DEAR xDRUMMER: Did you really used to play the drums? — *Spritely*

Yes, Spritely, I did . . . in a jazz band a long time ago.

Drummer, your photo looks very familiar, all but the white hair and beard. What did you do for a living?

Spritely, dear, I am a retired professor from the local university.

At "our" local university? Did you teach in the engineering department?

Yes, I did. How did you know?

Bill, is that you?
Yes, Spritely, but who are you?
My husband taught at the same university. Forty years ago we went to the same church that you and your family attended. My kids knew your kids. This is Betty Auchard.
Betty Auchard? Let me look at your photo again. By George, you're right! Why don't you have gray hair?
Bill, are you kidding? I color it.
Well, Betty, we've got some catching up to do. Let's meet for coffee real soon.
Sure thing, Bill. You name the place.
How about Thursday, 8:30 a.m., at the Coffee Roasting Company on Main Street?
Bill, we've got a date!

ProseChild (aka Texas Ray)

Hi, sugar, this is Texas Ray again, the guy who drills for oil and gas. How is your book going?
Hello, Ray. My book is almost finished. And how about yourself?
Well, sweet cheeks, I'm taking off a few months to work on my family history and enjoyin' every minute of it. What about your old violin? Did you ever find it?
Yes, Ray, I did. I actually found my dusty old violin case in one of the closets under a pile of worn-out blankets.
Sugar, tell me what it looks like and where it was made. Is there a date inside?
There is no date inside, but it was made in Germany and the strings are gone, the fingerboard is loose, the bridge is broken, and one of the tuners is missing. It's in complete disrepair. It really needs a lot of work. Do you think it's worth it?
Betty, there is not a violin around that can't be repaired if you're willing to take the time. What are you going to do with it?

Ray, I think I'm going to get this precious instrument re-glued, re-strung, and repaired so I can play beautiful music on it again.

You go, girl. Get a pencil and paper and I'll tell you how to go about that. Are you ready?

I'm ready.

[To be continued]

Epilogue

*L*ast week I asked myself an important question: "My book is finished. Where do I go from here?" My initial response was a lighthearted "wherever life takes me."

I know where I've been and how I got here. My journey through grief included occasional delays and setbacks, much like a board game. If I did everything right, I leap-frogged ahead six squares at a time. But whenever I forgot to pay a bill or missed an appointment, I ended up in the slammer for the next round.

Now that grief is behind me, I'd like to think that I have my act together, but apparently I don't. I recently went on a pilgrimage to Nebraska to visit family, make a presentation at a college reunion, and meet with *two* of my *three* editors named Sandy. While packing my suitcase for the trip, I remembered at the last minute that I had again forgotten to pay the bills. So I crammed things tight into my purse to make room for invoices, stamps, and my checkbook. I could easily accomplish that monthly chore during my two-hour layover in Las Vegas.

In the casino-type airport, I found a private table far away from the slot machines to shut out the clang of quarters tumbling into trays (no easy task) and concentrated on paying my bills. I addressed envelopes, slapped on stamps, and squeezed the bundle right back into my purse. How efficient and proud I felt for having used my time well.

Upon my arrival in Omaha, I asked Sandy (with a *y*) to drive past the post office so I could drop the paid bills into the curbside mailbox. What a relief to get that behind me! I had no idea I had also mailed my checkbook and receipts until I reached home nine days later and heard a friendly voice named Kathy on my answering machine. She was calling from the "Loose

Mail Department" in the Omaha post office. "Betty," said the voice, "because a thief has no doubt stolen your checkbook and discarded it in the mail box, I'll return it to you in California." What a surprise *that* was. I'm still getting loose receipts from the United States Post Office.

The frequency of my careless mistakes used to get me down, but not any more. I'm resigned to the fact that I sometimes move about in a haze and am a poor business manager and an even worse keeper of records. I would never make it as a secretary.

In spite of these minor distractions, I'm propelled forward by my excitement for the future and what it might hold. There are so many possibilities! I could return to a manuscript that I set aside three years ago, a collection of stories about being born in Iowa during the Depression and growing up during WWII. My parents loved each other, but couldn't stay together no matter how hard they tried. They married and divorced each other three times. My brother, sister, and I were often farmed out to relatives while my parents settled their squabbles. But my childhood was not as bleak as it might sound because my slightly dysfunctional family shared a lot of love and generated more than the average amount of excitement.

Maybe I'll finish the book I've barely started about my life as a nineteen-year-old bride in the small college town of York, Nebraska. I was housemother to twelve male students who were my own age and lived upstairs from my new husband and me. Their pranks made my life as a newlywed even more interesting than living with my parents.

I might write about entering public school teaching after earning a credential late in life. I call that my "gin and tonic phase" because other people's teenagers drove me to drink. But I adjusted, the administration kept me, and I taught art for twelve years.

I enjoyed teaching and creating art, but in the past five years, writing has become my focus. In the early weeks of my bereavement process when I saw no future ahead of me, I wrote, "Sometimes I wonder if I'll ever sew or cook again." The same is true now, but not for the same reasons. Now I wonder if I'll ever sew or cook again because I'm preoccupied with writing about the events in my life and the people who cause them. If I never had another story published, I would still write because it's as essential to me as eating and sleeping (and sometimes more so).

But as much as I love writing stories, my passion for telling them goes deeper. The people in an audience give me as much as I give them. We exchange energy. So I'll continue to accept every invitation to speak that comes my way — as long as I can work them into my social schedule.

Since I've joined several singles' clubs I have, at last, a social life that includes the male species. I'd almost forgotten men existed, but I began to miss them . . . terribly. Now I go on group dates just like I did in high school, and I'm having a wonderful time. But I don't neck in back seats anymore.

Life is certainly taking me to some interesting places. I've opened so many doors into my future that I have no idea which one I'll pass through first. I do know that I yearn to be in love again and to be loved in return. But maybe I should get organized first.